# AFRICAN
# SUMMER

~

*The Story of a
Fish out of Water*

~

ANDREW GILMAN

First published in 2013 by CreateSpace.

Printed in the United States of America.

ISBN-10: 1482731061
ISBN-13: 978-1482731064

*Dedicated to*
*Mighty and Bill*

# CONTENTS

# AUTHOR'S NOTE

This is a book about Africa, and a trip I took there in the summer of 2004. I was very young at the time, had never really traveled, and was far from worldly. I'm not saying I'm worldly now, but whatever I am is different. Africa will do that to a man.

That summer I spent seven weeks in the Gambia, one of those small places that usually escape the world's notice. The Gambia is called Africa's "Smiling Coast," and the people I met there were warm and welcoming. There were days of watching hippos in the river, drinking tea with silversmiths, and petting crocodiles under the burning sun. There were also termites in the food, and if that part was less than fun, the rest was beautiful. So this is a story of forgetting to look before you leap, and finding friends in unlikely places.

The names of some people in this book have been changed to protect their identities. Certain events, such as wild keggers involving several heads of state, have been omitted because to the best of my knowledge they never happened. And if they did, nobody invited me.

Enjoy.

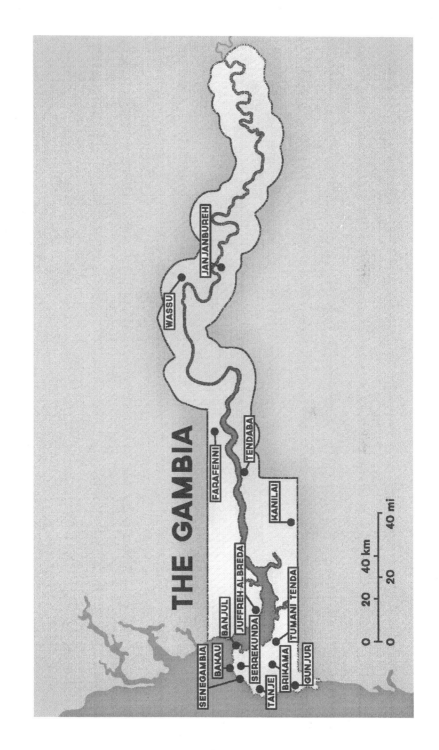

# CHAPTER ONE
# Into the Sky

If there was ever a man to take a trip like this, it wasn't me. Such were my thoughts as jets roared, pushing me back in my seat and lifting us from the runway till the plane slipped toward the stratosphere. Below, the crisscrossed terminals of John F. Kennedy International Airport faded in the gathering gray of a warm summer evening. New York City was already lost against the sky, and the light dimmed as we turned seaward, offered only a glimpse of dark blue before the bottom dropped out and we rose high in a starlit void. The butterflies in my stomach took flight with the plane, and despite the rising of my body, I had the sinking feeling I'd gotten into more than I bargained for.

To distract myself I took stock of my surroundings. I had a window seat right behind the engines, looking out on the shifting petals of the wing. I love window seats, with their view of the great nothingness through which you fly, and a wall to lean against if you can stand the engines' deep vibration. A window seat means your neighbors can only commandeer one of your armrests.

I needn't have worried about the armrests on this flight. My seatmates were two squat, Eastern European women, pleasantly helpful in their broken English, who seemed to sense I was out of my element.

Surroundings assessed, I took a deep breath, relieved to

be in the air. The road through Brooklyn had taken an eternity, long enough for those stomach-bound butterflies to grow exponentially, fluttering larger and larger with every minute we crept toward JFK.

It was hard to know what lay ahead. I was on my way to Africa, to a country called the Gambia, and that was *terra incognita* to me. We had a stopover in Madrid and a long layover in Francophone Senegal, but I'd forgotten my Spanish lessons and never learned a word of French. When we arrived in the Gambia we'd be there for seven weeks, studying culture, of all things. I wasn't sure why. So thank God there were — somewhere among the packed mass in that flying cigar — nine fellow voyagers bound for the same unknown shore.

• • •

As the engines settled into their long drone, I wondered what it was that got me on this plane. Was it bravado? Bravado had taken those last steps down the gangway to the jet — bravado and the knowledge that my parents had already invested thousands of dollars in this trip and would be waiting at the terminal gate if I turned around.

No, I thought as I hunkered down, it wasn't bravado alone that got me there. I was at the end of a long chain of events that led me to the plane, sitting next to two women chattering animatedly in Russian or Czech or some such. I had to look further than the gangway, further than the car ride through New York, back to when I started college and it all began.

I'd been attending freshman registration, feeling just about as green as could be, when I wandered into a film screening in the college auditorium. They were showing a documentary called *Tubabs in Africa*, made earlier that year during the college's summer field school in the Gambia. I don't remember why I went into the fateful screening. Perhaps something in the film's name — *tubabs*, which came from a West African term for white foreigner — caught my eye. Nothing else in my life hinted that I would be one to sign up for seven weeks in Africa. Up to that point I'd never been particularly adventurous, and spent most of my first eighteen years sitting quietly in the back of classrooms, trying not to say anything.

But that's one of the essential elements of travel. It pushes you beyond your boundaries, and shows you something new. When the film ended, the image of smiling students, teeth bright against tanned faces, stayed in my mind. Students who had taken the study tour spoke about their experience, and I hung on every word. The chance to spend almost two months studying culture in the tropics, surrounded by new sights and sounds... I'd never even heard of the Gambia, but now I couldn't think of anything better than exploring it.

I followed one of the students out of the auditorium, latching onto his arm as he tried in vain to escape. He only made it when I saw my father waiting and gleefully went to tell him of my plans to visit Africa. Two years before I set foot there, I was ready. Nothing in my life led up to that, but everything afterward followed.

Despite my enthusiasm, I had little chance to think about Africa in those early days. I majored in biology, concerned more with lab data than foreign cultures, but the images of the Gambia stayed with me. When I decided to major in anthropology during sophomore year, the trip suddenly fit. The stereotypical anthropologist is someone who goes into the bush armed with a tape recorder and notebook, finds a "primitive" tribe untouched by "civilization," and lives in a hut for months studying their "pristine" culture. At the end of this research period the anthropologist emerges, takes a much-needed bath, then lectures and writes about his experience "in the bush" for the rest of his natural-born life. It's hard to have a normal conversation with these people, because they feel obligated to remind you that they've roughed it and learned many interesting things, which they will be happy to share whether you like it or not.

I took my first anthropology class with Bill, the man in charge of the Gambia program, and he fit this description pretty well. He spent most of his time wearing dashikis and talking about Africa, all his classes descended into discussion on the Gambia sooner or later, and it wasn't long before I began to pepper him with questions.

My parents took a dim view of all this. The average American never goes to Africa, and in their minds it was a land represented only by images of violent street fighting and bloody coups. But that was what made it so appealing. I wanted to try and get a glimpse of lives that were nothing like mine, to see what it was like on the other side of the world. I wanted to see something different. Living in suburbia my entire life, I had no idea how people lived in Africa, or anywhere else in the world. I was attracted to the myth of Africa — the unfathomable continent that has defied explanation for centuries and even now exists as a monolith in the American mind. Was it real? Could I find it, or would it leave me dying of malaria like Dr. David Livingstone?

Every traveler has an image in mind when setting out, be it for the most familiar spot or the most foreign. Often it's this image that drives us, this picture of a place we dream of, calling us onward toward whatever we're seeking. I was seeking the exotic. Experienced travelers might disdain the term, but it still held value for me, as someone who was new at this, someone who hadn't had a chance to become jaded. Someone fresh off the boat.

In the meantime, I had to convince my parents it wasn't all insanity — something I wasn't too sure of myself. They'd known about my plan since the day I walked out of the screening and stated it in no uncertain terms. I think they dismissed it as a passing fancy, sweeping it under the rug and hoping I would do the same. But soon I dragged it out from under the rug and dusted it off, holding it up like a dead mouse and asking my parents to kiss it.

"You've never even been out of the country," said my mother, seeing the mouse.

"That's not true. I've been to Canada."

"You were four," they said, and I agreed this was true.

"You've never traveled alone," said my father, who joined the army and went to Korea straight out of college, but now thought this was a bad idea. "Maybe you should mull it over again. Have you really thought this through?"

"Sure I have," I said, telling them I'd considered it for the last year. This was a bald-faced lie. I'd made up my mind from the beginning, and rationalized the decision since then, but decided to go on record as having carefully considered my choice.

Privately, a very small voice said they might be right. Despite my bravado, I didn't know what I was doing, and imagined getting lost in an airport, winding up on a plane to Tokyo without even knowing it. I imagined being eaten by lions, trampled by a runaway rhinoceros, or ending my days in any number of equally colorful fashions. Maybe I was in over my head, but if I wanted to find something wild, something I had never seen before, Africa seemed like a good place to start looking.

"Couldn't you at least look at programs in safer places?" said my parents, growing increasingly desperate. "Like Cuba?"

I thought they were joking, but soon they flooded me with flyers for a country where the only things the government can't regulate are sex and marijuana, a place where people stay home on vacation to smoke pot and have sex. "A fine substitute for the Gambia," I thought as I tried to reason with them.

"It's not so bad," I said. "They'll give me pills for malaria, and a shot for yellow fever, and I can always bring a water filter, and... I'm not helping my case am I?" Horrified looks were their only reply, but they had raised a stubborn son.

Showing them *Tubabs in Africa* helped win them over, and once they saw the country onscreen, many of their fears dissipated. The Gambia was notably not on fire, and there were no soccer riots or coups in the background. They still seemed convinced I would die shortly after landing, but a combination of grim determination on my part and grim acceptance on theirs wore resistance down to the point where they buckled and said yes.

That took care of my parents. All that remained was to get a passport and visa, find the necessary medications, shop for supplies, and arrange transportation. I began to whimper when I looked at the mountain of work remaining, remembering why I'd taken always the easy path through life.

Getting the medications I needed didn't prove too difficult: a shot for this, a pill for that, and the usual "try not to die" speeches from my parents. Even if they felt better about the Gambia, malaria and other diseases still lurked. The passport and visa were also easy. A few forms, a photo, and I had my first passport. I felt sophisticated in a way I'd never felt before, and couldn't wait for those first entry stamps.

When it came time to book my flight, I endured countless lectures on the logistics of any trip to the Dark Continent, until I was able to book a ticket on the same flight as a professor joining the study tour. Following her seemed like my best shot at making it to the Gambia and not, for example, to Mongolia. Iberia Airlines would take us from New York to Madrid and then on to Dakar, capital of Senegal. Air Senegal would carry us the rest of the way, on the short hop down the coast to the Gambia. Others signed up for the same flights, and by the time the wheels left the ground ten people were there to support each other as we started into the unknown. I don't know what my parents were so worried about.

• • •

I woke early the morning after we left New York, still wedged in my seat beside the now-snoring Eastern European ladies. I'd barely slept during the night, anxious to be arriving in a strange land. Now Spanish hills rolled on beneath us, silent and golden in the morning sun, the brown earth ridged with valleys of shadow.

My ears popped as Madrid appeared in the distance, a sprawling mass among the hills. The airport was one giant crescent with moving sidewalks along the rim, and I walked through it with the anxious air of someone not used to travel, looking at every foreigner as if he or she was a criminal just waiting for the earliest opportunity to steal my money. Since we were in a crowded European airport, this meant I gave a lot of people strange looks. They returned the look whenever I tried to reach the money belt I'd shoved down my pants, far enough that in order to retrieve it I had to perform a maneuver that might seem highly suggestive without the proper context.

My bag weighed as much as a small elephant, and the moving sidewalks proved absolutely necessary. This is what happens when you pack for the unknown. I've heard it said that by basic economic standards, the best person for the economy is a terminally ill cancer patient undergoing a costly divorce. They spend the most, but I'm sure someone outfitting for Africa runs a close second. I'd personally packed enough to outfit a small safari, and had supplies for every problem — everything short of a civil war — that I could possibly encounter.

"What kind of equipment are you looking for, sir?" one of the salesmen had asked when I raided the local outfitting store, radiating an aura of an explorer in the making. He seemed to sense that I wanted to go for broke on my parents' tab.

"Sturdy stuff," I said. "Money's no object, my parents are paying." I saw a gleam in the salesman's eye when I explained my trip, and the rest of my shopping followed a well-defined pattern. He showed me a mosquito net or a water filter, I nodded thoughtfully and my parents nodded, asking if I wanted just one or would rather get three, and it seemed like we bought a dozen of everything just to be safe.

Louis Pasteur wrote that chance favors the prepared mind. I don't know about my mind, but my luggage was certainly prepared, and by the time I crammed it all into a backpack and two duffel bags, I started to think that chance might have to take a back seat to the laws of physics. I knew I would face something different than my usual fare, but thought I might have overdone it as I listed to one side like a sinking ship, staggering through the airport and looking for a place to put my bag.

We spent the afternoon in the Parque del Buen Retiro, taking the gleaming Madrid metro to relax in the park's shaded lanes, enjoying the quiet caused by a royal wedding somewhere else. The celebration meant the metro was free, but it also meant the shops in the park had closed, and when it began to rain we retreated to the airport, finding a quiet corner and settling down on hard plastic seats.

This was my first real chance to get to know my fellow travelers. Most of them had gone to informational sessions about the field school, but the most time I'd spent with them before landing in Madrid had been at the terminal in JFK. Now we took turns sleeping and guarding our bags from strangers.

There was Mary, who looked distinctly Irish, and made me wonder how she'd fare in the hot African sun. I took an immediate liking to Casey, a pretty girl with auburn hair and freckles all over. Most of the girls were anthropology majors, but there were some exceptions. Amanda, the only black girl on the trip, majored in chemistry. Sarah, Holly, and Aurore were all psychology students traveling with Debbie, a willowy professor with dark hair and bright blue eyes. The only one I really knew before leaving America was a man named Zach, and he wasn't on our flight. We'd shared a class that spring, and what I remember of our relationship up to that point was a series of sarcastic comments and sardonic grins. We would be roommates in the Gambia, and rooming with him for seven weeks promised to be interesting. Two girls named Abby and Christina rounded out our group, leaving us with a grand total of eleven travelers (and Bill, who waited somewhere in the great unknown). Together we dozed and paced, still nervous, unsure about what lay ahead. I might have been the least well traveled of my companions, but none of us had been to Africa.

Overhead, speakers announced calls for boarding, security advisories, and reminders about smoking. Our corner of the terminal had one of the designated stands for those who badly needed a cigarette break, and every once in a while we saw harried-looking people huddled around the stand like wanted fugitives, taking desperate pulls on their cigarettes and peering out at the rest of us. Christina and Abby joined in, both declaring that they wanted to quit but hadn't had much luck.

I read a little, and went to visit Abby and Christina in their smoke-filled exile, but I was exhausted from the restless flight and the long walk through the park. I took my shoes off, put them in my backpack so no one could steal them, and lay down on a row of seats with my pack as a pillow, feeling the hard seat ridges dig into my back as I drifted off to sleep.

"Andrew, get up!" The voice cut through my dreams, and I wanted it to go away. But it didn't, it just kept telling me to get up, get up, get up, until I opened my eyes and saw the girls standing over me, looking down expectantly.

"Is it time to go?" I groaned, wishing I were still asleep. My back hurt, and my body felt battered, barely refreshed by the nap. I groaned again and wondered vaguely where my shoes were.

"Yeah man," said Abby, her hands on her hips, her face a mask of perplexed impatience. "You're a really deep sleeper. We've been trying to get you up for ten minutes."

•  •  •

Leaving the Iberian Peninsula, we flew over rugged mountains, their crags grabbing at the cerulean sky. Everything looked parched, and isolated houses nestled in the brown landscape, seeking what shade they could as every building stood out against the background of bare earth.

Most of the other passengers were Africans, with a few European tourists sprinkled in. I heard Spanish, French, and German muttered about, but for the most part the cabin was silent, save for the rumbling of the engines. I drifted off to sleep soon after we left Spain, and when I woke I looked down through the tiny window and saw long, undulating lines on a dull brown expanse. I thought they were waves on the ocean, turned brown by some trick of the atmosphere, and wondered why they didn't move. Gradually it dawned on me that they were gigantic dunes draped on the Saharan sands. They rolled on in endless waves as far as I could see, receding into the distance under a dusty haze.

This must have been somewhere over Morocco or Mauritania. I was too tired to tell, and kept slipping in and out of consciousness, waking only occasionally for meals, devouring the food quickly and pushing it aside so that I wouldn't make a mess in my sleep. The sun set as we sailed above the cloud cover, and brilliant orange lit up the horizon, settling into red and finally purple hues. Then darkness fell around our plane and left us riding in an abyss.

In the pitch black ahead, Dakar shone like so many twinkling jewels. We came in across the water, and the waterfront sparkled as the continent rose to greet us. As I exited the plane, a wave of humid air rolled over me and I went out into the African night, leaving the plane under yellow floodlights and hustling across the tarmac into the confusion of the airport, where we had no idea where to go or what to do.

Nobody around us spoke English. We stumbled through immigration with the endearing air of travelers hopelessly out of their element, confronted by bored officials who took our passports and stamped them without a second glance. At the baggage claim we saw a man holding a sign with the name of our college, and some of us approached him while the rest went to get their luggage. We latched onto him like a drowning man grabs a lifesaver, but he didn't speak any English, either.

"*Français?*" he asked us hesitantly. We shook our heads. "Wolof?" he asked, naming one of the local languages. We shook our heads emphatically.

"Does anyone speak any French?" I asked the students near the baggage claim. The pretty girl named Aurore said she did, and became my new favorite person.

"Aurore, get over here! Speak French to this guy!"

With his help we made it through customs, past metal detectors that weren't plugged in, and out of the airport, where a mob immediately assailed us, yelling and trying to tear our bags away. They weren't trying to steal them — at least most weren't. They simply wanted to be porters so badly they abandoned all manners and forced their attentions on the white people. It wouldn't be the last time.

Out of the darkness came our savior, a Senegalese student named Honorine. She knew Bill, who had asked her to act as our contact in Dakar, and spoke English, which was the salient point. Brushing aside the crowding porters, she shepherded us to a waiting bus and hustled us aboard, urging "Go, go," as burly men threw our luggage on top.

We drove through black streets, a jumble of yellow lights in soft darkness, and the warm air wafting through the bus brought strange smells to us: the salty ocean nearby, roasting meat, and the reek of waste. Honorine handed out bottles of water, explaining that it was safer than drinking from the tap. We gulped gratefully, dehydrated by the long flight and the heat of the night, and I wondered if we would drink from bottles for the rest of the trip.

Somewhere in the darkness we came to the Ocean Hotel, our haven for the night. Bare yellow bulbs flickered over snaking corridors, and the tile floors were chipped in many places. We milled about the entrance, peering into the darkened dining hall, with its specials chalked up in a doorway crowded by leering masks. I was off in a corner by myself, and before settling in I told Debbie not to leave me behind in the morning. I was terribly afraid they'd take off if I slept in, and Debbie was clearly going to be the responsible one in our group. I knew she wouldn't forget.

My room had a single dim bulb overhead, an air conditioner in the window, and a working toilet in the rough bathroom. The shower had no curtain, and I soaked the bathroom cleaning myself, but it was worth it. The pillow on the bed felt hard as a rock. Bill had warned us about African pillows, which can be used to kill a man, but I was tired enough not to mind, and fell asleep almost instantly, the hum of the air conditioner lulling me to dreamland as cool air drifted down over me.

• • •

I woke up eager for the new day, unable to remember the

last time I rose at the mere hint of an alarm. I really didn't want to get left behind.

When I sallied out into the bright sunshine and poked around for breakfast, I realized how aptly named the Ocean Hotel was. Snow-white cloths covered tables on a shady veranda, looking out at the crashing surf of an azure sea. The coastline stretched out in the sun, tan buildings rising on darker rocks above the spray of rolling waves, and puffy clouds sailed across the sky overhead. It was delightful.

For all the luxury setting, breakfast was a simple affair of orange juice and bread. After eating, one of the girls started to pay with her left hand, and the rest of us hissed at her to stop and switch the money to her right hand. Honorine appeared and explained that the left hand is considered dirty in Senegal — and in most of Africa — where it is traditionally used to wipe after using the toilet. While the original reasoning may no longer matter in urbanized areas, the tradition remains strong. Eating, paying, or receiving money with the left is frowned upon. We laughed at this, but did our best not to offend anyone. Sometimes it made eating difficult, and more than once I found myself sitting on my hand to keep from insulting our hosts.

In the sunshine, Dakar looked more like a broken jumble of pale cement than the city of lights we saw the night before. The road was bumpy, its edges covered in blowing sand, and tall office buildings seen from the seaside became invisible once we descended into the belly of the city, winding through rough streets and out onto the flat expanse that led toward the airport.

I'd only spent the night, but I was reluctant to leave Dakar. It seemed exotic and fascinating, part of a different world. I'd be back before too long, on a trip at the end of the field school, but for now my mind was occupied by thoughts of what lay ahead.

At the airport we passed through a checkpoint, and

Honorine left us. Without a ticket, she wasn't allowed in. We waved goodbye and thanked her for saving us the night before. With Honorine gone, we were forced to rely on our Francophone guide and Aurore's shaky French to check the luggage, a process that involved arguing over regulations nobody seemed to remember. The words flew back and forth without much progress, as gendarmes came and went, then came back, and the men at the ticket counter rolled their eyes. I wished I knew French. I felt remarkably useless, standing by like a mute with nothing to say that could possibly help.

Finding our terminal was easier. There were only two of them to choose from, and the waiting area was almost empty when we arrived. Gradually it filled with bulldog men in business suits and round women in bright, colorful dresses, who sat in the rising heat looking grumpy and impatient, fanning themselves with magazines.

After an hour or two the announcers called us out to a small prop plane waiting on the tarmac. The flight lasted briefly. We followed a coast of stark beauty, its rock and sand set against the deep blue of the Atlantic, and as we turned downward to land I saw a white building standing alone in an empty field. The sharp edges of Yundum International Airport jutted into the sky, making it look like some space-age creation. Small wonder, when the United States government had invested in the airport as a possible emergency-landing site for the space shuttle. All the investment amounted to was a safety net at the end of the tarmac — which had never been put to the test — and as we bounced down I wondered if the net could stop a plane.

The sparkling cleanliness inside the building was a relief after the dusty tan of Dakar's airport. Everyone spoke English, and that was an even more welcome change. The Gambia had been a British colony, and if I didn't quite feel like saying "pip-pip, cheerio," at least I could get around without having to rely on Aurore for translation.

My luggage arrived safely, save for a handle missing from a duffel bag. Was it sailing through Spanish skies right now, or sipping a martini on the French Riviera? I had no time to wonder. We were finally there, and Bill waited for us behind customs.

"Glad you could make it," he said, a wide smile breaking the tan on his face. He wore a dashiki and looked perfectly at home.

Stepping from the air-conditioned chill of Yundum into the bright sun was a transition into another world. The light was almost blinding, and what previously seemed a dream became reality. I saw green taxis waiting, their drivers slumped in the shade, and chalk on a blackboard showed prices to towns near the capital city of Banjul, their strange names unfamiliar to me. Bill led us past the taxis, and we climbed into a waiting minibus, eager to reach our hotel and rest. As the van started up and pulled out onto the road, I knew we had embarked on a seven-week journey that would change us all. The Gambia waited.

## CHAPTER TWO
# Friendship

A long, lonely road led out from Yundum to the real world, and the airport seemed alone, half part of Africa, half part of something bigger.

Eager for my first real glimpse of the Gambia, I sat up front as we roared away, staring out at the land. It looked parched. The dry season was in full force, and the rains were overdue, so there was good reason for the beating sun and cracked earth. Mammoth termite mounds rose from the dust, and short trees broke the blue skyline with their deep green, dwarfed by thick baobab trees that towered over everything, their swollen trunks and twisted branches looking like roots that had lost their way. The baobab's strange appearance gave birth to a legend that the devil stuck it in the ground upside-down, and looking at it now, I felt inclined to agree. The harsh, rugged beauty of the land took us in, told us here was something real, something pulsing with vibrant life in spite of the merciless sun.

Slowly buildings appeared: rough, unfinished blocks of cement with shining metal roofs. Everything here was made of concrete, and with termite mounds curling around the trees, I could see why. The buildings crowded closer and closer as we drove into coastal towns, until finally we turned off the smooth asphalt road onto one rutted with potholes.

"We're really in Africa now," I thought as the bottom of the van clanged against the road. Ahead of us a large white building rose behind an imposing wall, and with a final bump our van rolled into the compound of the Friendship Hotel. It would be our home for most of the next seven weeks, and after driving through a land of little low buildings, I was glad to see something substantial waiting for us.

Guards lounged in the shade of a mango tree, resting beside the open gate. They didn't seem necessary, guarding the empty lots and dirt, but they looked very smart in their crisp uniforms. In the lobby, men in shirts and slacks and jeans slouched on a few battered couches. Their long pants seemed ill-suited to the heat, but Gambians are more formal than Americans when it comes to dress. Still, nobody could have paid me to wear formal clothes in the African sun. I was sweating in shorts and a t-shirt, and hadn't even bothered to bring long pants.

There were already several students at the hotel, enrolled in the college's semester program, but none showed themselves as I staggered up the stairs to my room. All the girls went to the second floor, but Bill apologized, said they had no rooms with the others, gave me a key for room 313, and promised he'd find one near the rest eventually. It didn't seem possible that all the other rooms were occupied, but the plumbing only worked in half of them.

In the brief interval between Madrid and Banjul, I'd forgotten how much my bags weighed, and now I gasped under their weight. As soon as I opened the door I dropped them with a loud crash, thinking that duffel bags should never be heavy enough to crash, and took a moment to survey my new home. The Friendship towered over the rest of Bakau, the coastal town sprawled around it. The People's Republic of China had built the hotel and the adjacent Independence Stadium, and the Friendship suffered from typical Communist architecture, only slightly offset by palm trees swaying over its central pool. Someone down there shouted at children as they splashed around the pool, their laughter filling the air. Smudges marred the robin egg blue of my room, and mosquito nets hung above its twin beds. A phone that didn't work sat on a table, and a small television perched high on a wall, displaying only static when I switched it on. Some of the static resembled a soccer game.

The room's balcony overlooked the hotel entrance, but the balcony door refused to open, even though I banged on it, shoving and working up a sweat. A small air conditioner stuck out of the wall, and I switched it on full blast, sitting on the bed in front of it and shivering as sweat evaporated. Whatever the hotel's other faults, the room was soon cold enough for any American.

We ate lunch in the hotel's dining hall, a cavernous chamber devoid of other customers, where we gulped ice-cold water gratefully and the kitchen staff set out a buffet: salad, black-eyed peas, fresh-caught fish from the nearby sea, and pineapple for dessert. I tried the fish, and after a bite or two my mouth burned, hotter and hotter the more I chewed.

"Hot, hot," I gasped, reaching for bottled water. I wasn't used to Gambian cooking, with its love of spicy foods and the taste of habanero peppers. The fish tasted excellent, just incredibly hot, and though my stomach growled, I couldn't manage more than half of what I put on my plate. My mind was still in America, where it was easy to be picky, and Gambian food would take some getting used to.

When lunch ended, I remembered I needed to call my parents. They made me promise to call the moment I arrived in Africa, and seemed to think I would find a way to call before getting through customs. That was hours ago. They probably thought I was dead by now.

Still, I was used to them worrying no matter what. They'd made me promise to call when I went to Michigan on a school trip, when they could simply have kept an eye on the news. If a group of college students goes missing in the middle of America, it will only be a matter of minutes before the media converge on their last known location and begin asking *why*. But this was Africa. You could probably go missing and not have your absence noticed for weeks.

Unfortunately, I had no idea how to phone home. Bill offered to take me into town to find a call center, and after taking a moment to wonder what that was, I ran to the room to get some money. At my door stood a short man with a scraggly goatee, dressed in a tank top and running shorts. He carried a bundle of sheets, and seemed to want into my room.

"My name is Mighty," he said by way of introduction. "I am here to help."

"Okay, nice to meet you," I mumbled, not at all sure I believed him. He was a complete stranger, and who has a name like Mighty? But I opened the door, and he grinned broadly, showing off bad teeth as I took the sheets, ushering him quickly out of the room. When he was gone, I locked the door and went into the bathroom, taking out the pills that were supposed to prevent malaria.

"Now, Andrew," the doctor had said when he gave them to me. "This stuff isn't one hundred percent effective. Chances are slim, but you can still get malaria."

"Then give me something better," I protested.

"I'm sorry, that's the best we can do."

"Great," I had thought as I pocketed the prescription. It never occurred to me that we hadn't found a cure for malaria, a disease with over two hundred million cases a year. He'd given me mefloquine, also known as Lariam, a common prophylaxis. Taken once a week, the pills destroy parasites that make their way out of the liver — but leave the ones in the liver intact. This medicine doesn't so much destroy the invading army as pick off the stragglers, and those stragglers come from one nasty disease. The mosquito-borne parasites that cause malaria can attack the liver, kidneys, and brain, causing anything from fever to coma — and, of course, a profoundly unpleasant death.

"And there are some possible side effects," continued the doc. Of course there were. There are always side effects, and avoiding them was now my main concern. "You may have weird dreams."

"My dreams are always weird."

"You might feel paranoid, anxious, and nervous."

"Doc," I said, "I'm heading to Africa. How do think I'm going to feel?" He regarded me with a smirk, as if to say I couldn't complain now, because this was all my idea in the first place. So now I downed the pill, hoped I wouldn't become any more paranoid than usual, and grabbed what I needed from the room before running to meet Bill.

Amanda and Debbie joined us as we piled into Bill's car, a rattletrap station wagon that wobbled violently from side to side. How many owners had abused it before it came to Bill? It shook so badly we dubbed it the "shimmy mobile," but despite its handicaps, the car got us down the road and into Bakau, a rambling collection of compound walls, small storefronts, and dirty back streets that ran smack into the Atlantic. Bill drove cautiously, which seemed wise. In some parts of Africa you had better not stop after causing an accident, mob justice being what it is. It was hard to imagine Gambians being that violent, but the road was not without its hazards, and every so often a goat darted into our path.

We drove past a mosque, its short minaret spearing the sky, but everything else squatted low, and after bumping over a potholed road to the sea, we stopped near a taxi park full of beat-up old taxis. Ramshackle stalls squatted across the street, filled with bright displays of tourist trinkets, and a small man ran out of one, approaching us eagerly.

"You come in, take a look," he said, pointing to the open storefront. "Just one minute!"

"We're too busy now," said Bill, waving the man away. "But listen, we'll come back later."

"You'll come back?"

"Yeah, we're just going over here, we'll be back." Bill gestured down the street.

"We're not really coming back, are we?" I asked when we were out of earshot.

"Sometimes you just have to lie," said Bill. "Or use humor, you know, joke with them." I nodded, agreed that this seemed like a perfectly fine way of dealing with strangers, and made a mental note that I would probably be lying a lot more than usual.

Next to the taxi park a faded sign indicated a GamTel (Gambian Telephone) call center. A fat woman in a bright dress sat behind a desk inside. She seemed comatose, but I roused her enough to explain that I needed to call America, and she gestured wearily toward one of the booths at the back of the room. Then she went back to sleep.

It took a minute to calm my mother down enough to get a word in edgewise. I let her know that a lion hadn't devoured me yet, and rejoined the others outside, just as eager to see more of the town as they were. The other new-comers and I followed Bill blindly, skirting the stall with the waiting salesman. The Atlantic lay beyond the trinket shops, and the view opened up when we reached a small beach.

A few colorfully painted boats rested on the sand, but it was the middle of the day and most of the fleet was out at sea. Our arrival quickly brought crowds of hangers-on, following us and calling hello, demanding that we buy smelly fish and asking pointed questions about Debbie and Amanda. They didn't quite know what to make of Amanda, unsure whether to call her "Gambian sister" or "*tubab*."

A lone pier of rusty metal grates stuck far out into the Atlantic, breaking up the perfect blue of sky and sea, and we walked to the end, enjoying a quiet moment away from the friendly locals before returning to the Friendship. Halfway out, a fisherman sat mending his nets, checking for tears, but between fishing and tourist dollars it was easy to see which won out. Bakau was a popular tourist spot in the Gambia, and from the pier I could see the seaside fronts of unfinished hotels.

Back at the Friendship, I stretched out on the bed and promptly went to sleep. The foam mattress and hard pillow were uncomfortable, but the combination of jetlag and hot sun made them infinitely appealing.

Sometime later I woke in darkness, still tired but no longer exhausted. Disoriented, I glanced at my watch, noting that it read eight o'clock, and hoping it meant eight in the evening I stumbled down to the dining hall, praying there would be food.

Everyone already sat around the tables, including a few of the semester students staying at the hotel. Zach, the last of our group to arrive and the man who would be my roommate for the remainder of the trip, had finally appeared. I said hello to the gathered *tubabs*, took an empty seat and asked Zach when he got in.

"A while ago," he said, grinning through his beard.

"And you didn't even get me up for dinner?" I glared at him and Bill.

"We tried," said Bill. "We pounded on your door, but we couldn't wake you up. We had to put Zach's stuff in my room."

"Bullshit, I don't sleep that heavily. And I was tired."

"Dude, we pounded on the door for ten minutes," said Zach.

"Well, I was *very* tired," I said, feeling suitably chastened. "Sorry."

The food was still spicy, and I nibbled at it before re-treating to bed. Even after the nap I was tired enough to pass out almost immediately, knowing we had a full day ahead. It wouldn't be the last busy day, or the last time I locked Zach out of the room.

## CHAPTER THREE
# Tubabs

Monday was our first day of classes. I woke at seven, a phenomenon that wouldn't be repeated, not if I had anything to say about it, and hurried down to greet my fellow travelers. They huddled over tables in the dining hall, chewing on greasy fried eggs and baguettes, drinking glasses of Tang orange drink. Gambian cooking, perfectly suited to lunch and dinner, left something to be desired early in the morning.

Bill introduced us to the hotel staff, though I couldn't imagine how to spell some of their names. I wrote them down as best I could, but probably got most of them wrong. I hope they'll forgive the slight. There was Mr. Chaum, general manager at the Friendship, who seemed friendly and helpful. Malik Ceesay was in charge of beverages, and Chef Omar Szo commanded the kitchen. I would have to talk to them about the Tang. Sake Bure looked after the hotel's safe, which I declined to use on the grounds that I still had my money belt stuffed deep within my pants. "Mighty" Hatabu Sanneh, the man I'd met the day before, was an assistant for the program and there to help us with anything we needed. Lastly we met Kawsu Ceesay, an older man who spent his days supervising the pool, keeping it relatively clean when he wasn't yelling at small children.

The sheer variety of Gambian names made it hard to

remember them all. The Christians we met took their names from the New Testament, which made them familiar enough, and the Muslims took theirs from the big players in early Islamic history: Mamoudou, Amadou, and Ibrahim for the men, Issatou and Hazimatou for the women. Half the men I met went by Oumarou or Boubakar, leading to inane conversations as we tried to tell them apart:

"I saw Boubakar today."

"Pool Boubakar?"

"No, the other one."

"Oh, you saw market Boubakar?"

"No, no. Young Boubakar."

"Which one?"

These hasty introductions over, we took to the bus to visit the local American embassy. For some reason, we needed to register with the embassy — probably to avoid Americans disappearing abroad. It sat in a commercial strip along Kairaba Avenue, a busy road that seemed to encapsulate expat life in a row of embassies, supermarkets, and Internet cafes. Here was the place to buy liquor, cheeseburgers, and potato chips.

Inside the high palisade of the embassy, the staff sat us down to talk about not screwing up. This is something the American government takes very seriously abroad, and we met the embassy's regional security officer, a fresh-faced young man not much older than us, so he could deliver "the talk."

"The talk" consisted of warnings about wandering around at night or doing stupid things while drunk. I thought it would have been more effective if the officer giving it was a gruff, heavyset man with a crew cut and a drill sergeant manner, but this wasn't to be. Instead this young man chided us not to do anything we'd regret in the morning. I think everyone gets the same talk when they go away to college. The only difference was that here in Africa, they warned us to avoid foul water and take our pills. But this wasn't anything Bill hadn't told us already.

On an alternate route back to the hotel, we passed the low office of the Peace Corps. Bill had served as a volunteer in the Gambia decades before, and he pointed to the office with a certain amount of pride. I didn't see any guards, but perhaps they were hiding in the trees.

In a stuffy conference room that overlooked the hotel's dusty parking lot, we began classes when we returned to the Friendship. Bakary Sidibeh, a highly respectable Gambian of advancing years and slow speech, began to teach us the finer points of Gambian etiquette, aided by a man named Boubakar and a woman called Adam, a soft-spoken pair who would soon start teaching our language classes. We paid attention — nobody wanted to accidentally insult our hosts — but it was hard to absorb the subtleties of a new land in a classroom. People took off their shoes when entering a mosque, or when entering their in-law's house, which I didn't think would become an issue. Direct eye contact was rude in conversation, and I wondered what to focus on if I couldn't look at the person I was speaking to. We learned not to smell food before we ate it, and not to put our napkins in communal bowls when we finished. All this was easy to note down, harder to remember when it mattered. I left the session determined not to offend anyone, and when we went to lunch I sat on my left hand, just to be sure. Looking around, I noticed I wasn't the only one.

After lunch we stood in the sun and waited for language class to begin. The Gambia has a diverse range of ethnic groups, including the Mandinka, Wolof, Jola, and Fula, each with their own language. In spite of the country's low literacy rate, many Gambians are multilingual; having grown up exposed to so many different tongues, it was only natural for them, and now was our chance to catch up. We could choose either Wolof or Mandinka for the first two weeks of our study tour — hardly enough time to properly learn the language, but maybe enough to say, "Now that I've married your daughter, I'm taking off my shoes when I enter your house." The Mandinka were the most numerous ethnic group in the country, but Wolof was more common near the coast, where it served as a lingua franca for the various groups. I thought it would be good to speak the most common language, and waited in the conference room for Mandinka class to begin.

"*Salaam aaleekum*," said Adam when she entered, meaning "peace be upon you." That first greeting wasn't Mandinka at all, but Arabic, and sufficed for a common greeting in the predominantly Muslim Gambia. Adam wrote out the response phonetically, matching the Arabic sounds to "*maleekum salaam*," or "peace be unto you also." There was also a Mandinka greeting to ask if you're at peace, to which the answer was "peace only." And when we asked where the family was, "they are there" was the response. We hoped there was no trouble, and the reply of "no evil" set everyone at ease.

We spent the class reviewing our small list of exchanges, greeting each other over and over so that we became used to the strange sounds, but I could barely keep them straight. In my mind I heard Spanish phrases floating past. Flying through Madrid may have played a part, but it was something deeper than that. I was trying to learn a third language, and my brain reverted to patterns learned earlier in Spanish class. It made it hard to learn Mandinka when every time I tried to say "hello," a large part of me wanted to say "*hola*." Staring at the unfamiliar words, I concentrated on the Mandinka in front of me, pressing ahead as best I could and trying to ignore the foreign tongue I already knew.

The Wolof class seemed easier than ours. When the session let out they jabbered away with their new greetings, while we continually looked at our notes. Maybe I was just dense, but I knew I'd rather enjoy the Gambian sunshine than study in it. Putting the notes in my room, I went to join the others, and promptly forgot to study them until class the next day.

• • •

"I've got some good news for you all," said Bill over dinner. "The president of the Gambia invited us to a party in honor of the outgoing American ambassador, and we're going tomorrow night."

"But Bill, I haven't a thing to wear," I protested, my voice rising with alarm. It looked like the decision not to pack formal clothes was coming back to haunt me, and I panicked, imagining being turned away at the door or left behind altogether. Gambians could be surprisingly stuffy about dress, considering the tropical clime they lived in.

I left the dining hall with a knot in my stomach, and there was more to it than simple worry about the party. Everything had to be figured out here, as if nothing worked the way I was used to. I'd begun to feel twinges of nervousness, and a gut feeling that something was wrong. It was a feeling that had nothing to do with this new party. I couldn't put my finger on the precise reason for my discomfort, but the Gambia made me sweat.

After dinner it was time to find other ways of contacting home. Snail mail seemed out of the question. The Gambian post office was better than many African countries' but still far from perfect. I never wrote letters in the States, and when it might take a week or two for a letter to arrive, it hardly seemed the time to start. Instead I joined Christina, Abby, and Zach as they wandered off to find an Internet café.

The warm night air enveloped us outside the hotel gates, and our path took us to the part of town that Bill drove through earlier. How different it looked at night, when the lights on the dark road stood out at long intervals, casting pale yellow beams across the street. They seemed like untouchable stars above high compound walls. As we walked by, calls of hello followed our steps, and I felt unnerved wandering in a strange place, with flashlights lighting up the dirt and trash at our feet, guiding the way as the occasional car barreled past.

I hadn't noticed many details of the town before, but we'd heard that a small café sat across from the mosque, and we wandered through the dark in that direction, until a few lights appeared, a sign advertised the Sweet Planet Internet Café, and a small knot of teenagers hung around the entrance. Inside the tiny room, there weren't enough open computers for all of us.

"Who wants to wait?" said Abby.

"I will," I volunteered reluctantly. "But you have to wait for me when you're done."

The rates were reasonable: half an hour cost ten dalasi, the local currency, which meant roughly thirty-three cents. As seats opened up, we paid and squeezed into place at old computers, where the figures on the keyboard were in Arabic. A dim light flickered overhead, completing the cheap ambiance of the dingy café.

In the Gambia, you get what you pay for, and I quickly learned why the price was so low. It took me most of the first half hour to get to the first website, and clearly more would be needed if I ever wanted to communicate at any great length. I dashed off a quick message to tell my family I was still alive, then gave up and left. I was the last of our small group to leave, and found the others waiting outside. None of us wanted to walk home alone.

# CHAPTER FOUR
# The Lucky Crocodile

I woke sometime after breakfast, aware of a rumbling hole where my stomach used to be. I was hungry, and sour because of it.

The key was still inside the door when I rose, which meant Zach hadn't been able to get in the night before. I had done it again, and pulled on my sandals just as I heard a knock at the door. When I opened it and let Zach into the room, he accused me of sloth, and I muttered something that wasn't very nice. I wasn't in a mood to apologize, but I felt like an ass.

"Are you all right Demba?" shouted Kawsu when I left the room, and I saw him waving where he sat in the shade, resting by the side of the pool.

"Yes, Kawsu, I am fine. How is the day?"

"Fine, Demba, fine!"

Kawsu had decided to adopt us all into his family and give us Gambian names to welcome us to the Ceesay clan. Zach was now Musa, and I was Demba. Someone told me the name meant "yesterday" in Wolof. I was glad he hadn't named me something like "fatty." One never knows with these things.

Hurrying to join the other students in class, I saw a face bobbing along the hotel paths, and did a double take. I was sure I recognized the man it belonged to, but hadn't expected to see him here, four thousand miles from home.

"Isaac," I shouted, and the face turned as I ran up to greet a friend I hadn't seen in months. He looked just as surprised as me, and asked what I was doing there.

"Studying, man. So this is where you've been? Hiding away in the Gambia?" I laughed, thumping him on the back as he grinned through his beard.

"You didn't know that?" he said, as if I were being dense on purpose. I hardly knew my fellow travelers before the trip, but had known Isaac since the first days of college, and it was good to have at least one friend in the Gambia.

"This is my girlfriend Becky," Isaac said, introducing a tall, slender girl with dark hair. Becky shook hands but made no sound, and her face remained locked in a frown.

"Jeez, she's not very friendly," I thought.

"Becky ate a green mango, had a bad reaction, and now she can't move her mouth," explained Isaac, and I felt like an ass for the second time that day.

• • •

Language sessions should never be attempted on an empty stomach, but that was what I found myself doing as I gathered my unstudied notes and joined the rest of the Mandinka speakers. We greeted each other — sometimes in Mandinka, sometimes in English — and then I fell asleep. Bakary Sidibeh was back for our cultural lesson and had a habit of wandering off topic, ignoring time constraints and dozing listeners as he went. I began to suspect that Gambian lecturers loved the sound of their own voices too much for their own good.

Lunch only made the grogginess worse, and I dozed through the afternoon sessions, drooling slightly in the heat. When I woke to find Zach staring at me, I realized we needed to get out of that room. It was hot, an open oven that made us sweat without any effort, and these classes weren't why I signed up for a trip to Africa. I wanted a change of scenery, a look at real Gambian life and not some dry talk on ancient history, so I breathed a sigh of relief when Bill led us out the gates, into the breezy freedom of Bakau, where whiffs of open sewer punctuated the smell of the sea. We held our breath and crossed the sewers, their black depths emanating a foul stench. Some parts of "real Africa" smelled sweeter than others.

We followed Bill through the broad streets, past goats frolicking on tree stumps and groups of schoolgirls in matching uniforms. Two men stood in a shack down the road, the bright blue lights of their arc welders casting showers of sparks on an unfinished steel door. I looked around, trying to get a handle on the Gambia. There was poverty, but it wasn't depressing, not like I'd expected it to be. I'd seen poverty before, and it was usually very depressing. The saddest place I've ever been was an old coal town in Pennsylvania, driving home on a bleak winter's eve, when the whole earth looked dead and gone, and the only color came from the neon beer signs in dingy bars.

The Gambia was different. I'd expected to feel pity. Americans are conditioned to look on Africa as a place to be pitied, and Africans as people to be pitied. But there was none of that here. The sun shone brightly. Children played in the street, laughing in carefree amusement. Old men in long robes sheltered in the shade, for even the receding afternoon heat was worth avoiding, and women chatted around cooking fires. There was plenty of food. Young men lounged under tall trees, though their leisure wasn't wholly voluntary, given a national unemployment rate of almost fifty percent.

It was hard to feel bad for people who looked so happy, and the Gambia is called the "smiling coast" with good reason. People everywhere were smiling and friendly. Everyone greeted us, said hello, and inquired after our health. Half of them then asked for money. It seemed like a peaceful country, a safe country, and I felt at ease despite the obvious differences between the Gambians and me.

The young men in the shade eyed the women walking by, calling out to them like raunchy construction workers. Several broke off as we passed, pursuing the girls in our group. None of the girls expressed any interest, a point lost on the men, who were smooth as bricks. Some of them looked like they'd also been hit with a brick, and a fair number hadn't heard of dental hygiene, judging by the lack of teeth and the smell of their breath.

As the roads narrowed and abandoned pavement altogether, we peered into compounds to catch a glimpse of daily life. Welded metal doors decorated the richer houses, and spikes topped their walls, while poorer houses had corrugated metal doors on rough wooden frames, and shards of broken glass took the place of spikes. Inside we saw bare courtyards with a few belongings: cooking pots, a stool in the shade of a banana tree, and possibly a squalling baby toddling across the sand.

Hidden among the squalor, we came suddenly to the sheltering quiet of Katchikally crocodile pool. A small, whitewashed hut guarded the entrance to the oasis, and the figure of a *kangkurao* greeted us inside. Clad entirely in a bark coat, the *kangkurao* is one of the most powerful spirits of West Africa, capable of killing cannibal-witches that torment innocent villagers. With their whips and machetes, *kangkuraos* serve as enforcers of tradition, given orders and tasks by the elders who summon them.

The strange costume seemed like a contradiction in a predominantly Muslim society. Strict Islam holds Allah alone as the sole supernatural power in the world, but a shrine in the corner held offerings to ancestors and spirits that live all around us, and I sensed the hold that history still had on modern Gambians. Where a Western museum would carefully stress how the artifacts came from the world of the distant past, there was no such distinction here. Tradition was alive and well.

A pair of bellows stood next to blacksmith's tools, looking like something from centuries ago, but I knew they still served their craftsmen in the Gambia, and looked forward to seeing them in action. One of the students in *Tubabs in Africa* worked with blacksmiths, and I'd talked to Bill about doing the same when it came time for independent research. I pictured myself pounding away at a forge, my face streaked with sweat, muscles corded and bunched, making an ax as red-hot sparks flew.

I was arrogant, thinking that I would learn the trade in a matter of weeks. But I was also attracted to the idea of the exotic artisan, toiling away in the manner of an ancient, a man using tools and traditions that his grandfather might have used. I wanted to find out how modern artisans lived, how they worked as the Gambia crashed into the future. First I needed a place to start, a contact, an informant, but that could wait, because right now I wanted to see the crocodiles.

Beyond the huts, a gaping hole sank in the earth. Pink and orange flowers hung lazily from the trees, adding their sweet perfume to the air, and roots crept out of the pit's walls, sloping down to a pool covered in green scum. The only things hinting at the water below were the leering eyes and toothy grins of partially submerged crocodiles.

As we sat by the pool an older man came to speak with us, dressed in the long robe known as a *boubou*, introducing himself as Ousman Bojang, caretaker of the sacred pool.

"Oh no," I thought, "another Gambian lecturer." Inwardly I groaned, but as he began to speak I was lost in the story of his family. Five hundred years ago the Bojang clan had wandered aimlessly, searching for a peaceful place, chased by enemies until they had nowhere to turn. Then the forest spirits of Katchikally offered to protect the people, if only they would stay and care for the pool. Since then the Bojangs have been the caretakers at Katchikally, looking after the pool and its reptilian inhabitants. Ousman's father had been caretaker, and the pool fell into disrepair after he died and Ousman moved away. The sides collapsed, the water table dropped, and many of the crocs disappeared. One year Ousman came back, found the pool almost filled with dirt and began to rebuild, fixing the walls, digging deeper until water filled the hole again.

With their home restored, the crocodiles returned, and among them was Charlie, the most famous crocodile in the Gambia. Touching him brought good luck, but the pool held its own healing powers, reputed to cure infertility in any woman who bathed in it. I thought that any woman brave enough to bathe with crocodiles deserved to have as many children as she wanted, and the women who'd been cured formed an extended family, supporting each other and coming to sing and dance at the pond.

I had a hard time not calling Ousman "Mr. Bojangles" as we walked down to the water. Gray crocs lounged in groups or sat like malcontents by themselves, and next to the pulsing neon algae, they seemed dull in comparison. None of them moved. To one side, a slender one slid out of the pool and collapsed on the shore. Then stillness reigned again.

"Charlie" sat on the shore, though I wondered if the Bojangs simply pointed at the nearest reptile and called him Charlie when visitors arrived. He seemed remarkably long-lived, even for a well-fed reptile. Moss covered the ridges on his back, and he grinned toothily at us. If petting him was the Gambians' idea of good luck, I wasn't sure I wanted any part of it. But he looked comatose, and after the third or fourth person rapped his back without him so much as batting an eye, it began to look less crazy. I started to think Charlie might be asleep, or dead and stuffed, in which case there was little danger in petting him. One by one the rest of us rapped his back and came away with our limbs intact. He must have been used to the attention: a nearby shack sold t-shirts, carvings, and necklaces, most of them adorned with his image.

Before we left we posed for pictures among the spreading roots of a cotton tree, squeezing side by side in the vast folds of its trunk. "The tree holds the spirits of the people who settled here and made this place," said Mr. Bojang, gazing up at the tree. "It is their house. It is their home. And they protect this place." In the peace and quiet of the tranquil forest, I could easily believe it.

## CHAPTER FIVE
# The Emperor's New Clothes

On our return from the sacred pool, the children of Bakau came out to join us. Some of them begged, but others just followed, tagging along until we had a constant group at our heels, holding our hands and quite content to walk with us wherever we were going.

"*Tubab, tubab*," called the children. "White man, white man."

I could only imagine how parents would react to such a sight in the States. A stranger, holding hands with their children and leading them down the street? There would be words exchanged, and probably a call to the police. No one in Bakau batted an eye. Children in the Gambia were freer than their American counterparts, more often left to their own devices. Unsupervised, they played in the streets, and it seemed a more innocent place because of it.

I still wondered what to wear to the president's party. In packing for the Gambia, I brought nothing for the formal ballroom, and as everyone else got ready that afternoon I borrowed slacks and a polo shirt from Bill, thinking that sandals would just have to do for footwear.

"Have you heard about this guy?" said Zach, reading about the Gambia's president as I dressed. "He took over in a coup, but it's like he and six of his army buddies just got tired of the president, and decided to overthrow him."

That wasn't entirely accurate, but it was close. On July 22, 1994, Colonel Yahya Jammeh and several of his fellow officers decided they'd had enough of then-president Dawda Jawara, and staged a bloodless coup. After the revolution, Jammeh set up a government headed by himself and the Armed Forces Provisional Ruling Council. He promised that the new government would, of course, be temporary. Then he began wearing aviator sunglasses and army fatigues at press conferences, making him a favorite of dictators the world over. The new leader either didn't notice the disdainful looks of Western leaders, or didn't care — at least until they pulled aid money from the country. By the time we visited he had decided to care, and the party for the outgoing ambassador seemed like evidence of a new attitude toward the donor nations of the West.

That night black faces shone in the lights of the Kairaba Hotel, one of the most expensive resorts in the Gambia, and the Gambia at night seemed to come alive with a strange energy, abuzz with festivity as well-dressed guests made their way inside, showing their invitations to security. A troupe of women sang an incomprehensible song of welcome by the door, and in the hotel courtyard soldiers strutted in olive green, or lounged around looking bored because they couldn't go and get drunk.

Inside, the country's elite sat at lavish tables, looking stiff and uncomfortable. Waiters scurried about in spotless uniforms, serving drinks, filling and refilling wine glasses. So much alcohol surprised me. I'd been told Muslims couldn't drink, but judging by the amount of wine flowing, few were letting that stand in their way. On a stage at the front of the room, a band of men in smart blue uniforms played the "Stars and Stripes Forever," and a long table at the back was set for the bigwigs. The president's space was noticeably empty.

Bill seemed to know everyone, and quickly mingled

with the ministers and officials as I sat down next to Isaac and Becky. Becky's mouth still didn't work, so Isaac did most of the talking, telling stories about their recent trip to Guinea and the trouble they had when they left their passports at the border.

When everyone was in their seats the president appeared, fashionably late and dressed in a flowing white robe, a carved wooden staff in his hand. Maybe his old uniform just didn't fit anymore. The emperor's new clothes matched his expanding girth, but the robe failed to hide his ample belly.

"Thank you, Your Excellency Doctor Alhadji Yahya Jammeh," droned a minister, "for this magnificent dinner party, which you have been gracious enough to hold for the American ambassador. A party for which you have graciously decided to postpone *your own birthday party…*"

A round of polite but not overly enthusiastic applause rippled through the crowd. The next man repeated the thanks and said he only wanted to emphasize how gracious Jammeh was to delay his own birthday celebration. The third said the same, and the one after that, and as I listened to official after official remind us of Jammeh's supreme generosity in holding off his birthday party, I reflected that he'd clearly learned the art of fawning over donors in the years since his coup.

When the president finally rose, he spoke about the magical bond between Gambians and their American brethren, their partnership in trade and peace, and about our college. He mentioned Bill by name.

"How small is this country?" I thought, pleased that he acknowledged us. I suppose it was the least he could do, after the college gave him an honorary doctorate for speaking at commencement the year before. He'd certainly taken to calling himself doctor with flair, and I wondered how much "legitimacy" we'd granted him by giving that title.

The bands took over when the president sat down, mixing martial music with dances and drums as the evening trailed on, until finally people began to leave and we filtered out. The bus waited in the crowded parking lot, engine idling as we climbed aboard and settled wearily into our seats.

"Mistah Gilmannn," said Mighty, who'd come with us to the party. He leaned toward me, grinning and reeking of alcohol, and I noticed the bottle of wine he'd secreted away from the banquet.

"Mighty, I thought Muslims couldn't drink," I said as we drove off into the night.

"Yes," he said, his grin growing even wider. "I am a bad Muslim!"

• • •

Our van sped toward the horizon the following afternoon, running along a long strip of highway that shone in the sun and led to the capital city of Banjul.

Previously known as Bathurst, administrative capital of Britain's Gambia colony, Banjul began in 1816 atop a spit of land on the coast, and the land grew swampy as we advanced, until a slender bridge appeared over a narrow band of water. Just before the bridge a blue-clad police officer stood at the window of a large van, examining the driver's papers. We'd seen several checkpoints on the road to Banjul, but none looked too impressive and we shot past, ignoring the officer, who barely glanced up at our passing. When a checkpoint consists of two bored-looking policemen on the side of the road, and all stops seem arbitrary, it begs the question of what happens if you don't stop.

"Oh," said Bill. "You keep going." Nothing got by Bill, and we looked at him blankly, asking if they might decide to give chase.

"It'd have to be on foot. They don't have police cars."

"But they could shoot at you, right?"

"Maybe, but they can only afford live ammo for half the guards."

That only raised the further question of whether or not they told the guards if they had live ammo that day. I could only imagine the conversation at the police station, the captain handing out live ammo to half his men and telling the rest to stay behind them.

We rushed across the bridge, glad we weren't on the skeletal span of an older bridge to seaward. On the other side, a canning factory reeked of fish, and boats bobbed at anchor in the water below. This wasn't the river that gave the country its name, just one of the myriad channels leading into marshes south of Banjul.

A beach appeared just past the bridge. Its pale sands stretched along the pounding Atlantic, and a cemetery stood near the sea, full of Muslim and Christian graves side by side, the differences of mortal ideologies forgotten in death. The graves were eroding into the sea. From the road we could see the outer edges sunk lower into the beach, gradually merging with the earth and dissolving into the sea.

Just beyond the dead, the statue of a soldier in combat fatigues, holding a child and giving a peace sign, guarded the outskirts of Banjul. Ostensibly known as "the unknown soldier," the statue looked like Jammeh in his younger, fitter, fatigue-wearing days — a reminder to the Gambian people of who rescued them from the last president's stagnant regime.

Part of the discontent with Jawara stemmed from the longevity of his reign. He became the Gambia's first president in 1970, and with that peculiar politician's instinct, decided to stay on as long as he could. Inertia and inactivity marked his administration, and the resulting discontent led a group of soldiers to attempt a coup in 1981. Senegal helped Jawara oust the men, and he continued to rule until the economy worsened and Jammeh took over in 1994.

Jammeh had been there for ten years when I arrived, and showed no signs of stepping down anytime soon.

Our van pulled off the road by a towering arch behind the statue. Built to commemorate the coup that brought Jammeh to power, Arch 22 was designed by Pierre Goudiaby Atepa, the Senegalese architect who designed Yundum International Airport, and was another reminder of the significance Jammeh placed on his revolution. He wanted a massive symbol to remind Gambians what they owed him. With its bold lines, the edifice had been designed to impress, but cracks in its surface and weeds at its base diminished the effect.

Still, the view from the top wasn't bad. The city stretched out toward the ocean — parliament buildings, government ministries, residences, hospitals — all of it far below. The only structures that rivaled the arch were the twin minarets of the King Fahad Mosque, towering above the rest of the city. Ninety percent of Gambians are Muslim, and mosques were everywhere, as ubiquitous as churches in America. The imam's call to prayer echoed over the city noise, but the call was in Arabic, and I had no idea what it meant beyond the opening lines of "*Allahu Akbar,*" God is greatest.

Banjul was small, and from the top of the arch we could make out ships at sea, passing slowly from the mouth of the Gambia River. The city proper held less than thirty-five thousand souls, though the greater Banjul area, including Bakau, had a population more than ten times that — almost twenty percent of the people in the country.

The coastal area around Banjul wasn't always the prominent part of the country. For years a region called Niumi occupied the center of power on the northern bank, ruled by kings who extorted tribute from a much larger area. The arrival of the British changed that. They'd contested the region for years with the French, but by 1889, when the

Gambia officially became a British Crown colony, Bathurst had gained significant power, enhanced by British views on how to govern the Gambia. To them, the area where government officials and expatriate traders lived was colony. The rest, over four thousand square miles populated almost entirely by Africans, was merely seen as protectorate, to be brought along more slowly than Bathurst. This set a pattern that continues today in the dominance of the capital region over the rest of the country, and its resulting growth with rural migrants.

It was a short ride from the arch to the National Museum. Run by the National Centre for Arts and Culture (NCAC), the museum housed a collection almost identical to the one in Katchikally: a few masks, a *kangkurao*, and a collection of faded photographs, half-forgotten in an airless back room, showing the old days of colonial rule. It was a place where history went to die, and we were the only visitors.

Outside, the top of a small hut formed a cage that held the museum's resident silversmiths. From it, the din of hammers rang across the courtyard, and Bill asked if I wanted to talk with the men. The last four weeks of our trip would be spent on independent research, and I still needed contacts if I wanted to study traditional artisans. So absolutely, I wanted to meet them.

Three men squatted inside the tiny enclosure: an older man, a middle-aged man, and a younger man, all pounding on anvils. They looked like animals in a cage, on display for tourist to gawk at. I tried not to gawk, and we asked if they would show me the ropes. The older man grunted and nodded, his grizzled head bobbing. I said I looked forward to working with him — whatever that might mean — but he was intent on the fine filigree in front of him, and I thought it best not to press the issue. Two weeks still remained before I would be left to my own devices, and I'd cross that bridge when I came to it.

That evening I played cards with Debbie, Abby, and Sarah, enjoying the cool of the African twilight. The speaker for dinner hadn't shown, and when we finished eating we left the empty dining hall for the quiet of the hotel's pool bar — a low building with rickety chairs and battered tables where we whiled away our free time. Sarah knew a few card tricks, showing us as dusk settled all around, the lights of the hotel shining softly into the darkness, and afterward it was a long time before I could force myself to sleep.

## CHAPTER SIX
# Drums in the Sun

Culture shock hit me like a prizefighter the next morning, and I woke with the urge to do nothing. This curious illness, pronounced in those who've never traveled, and eased in more experienced voyagers, still wasn't something I expected. But there was no denying it. My spirits flagged as our presenters droned on through the morning. The lecture room boiled, and I felt myself begin to stray, growing tired of the whole thing, not interested in this new culture or the people around me.

I didn't know what was wrong with me. Sure, I'd never been abroad, but I was a twenty-year-old college student. I thought I'd left all that teenage angst behind in high school, but the Gambia was bringing me so far out of my element, it was like adjusting to a new diet. And if I could be honest with myself, I was afraid — afraid of the unknown, of the unfamiliar, of the strange and the new. It was hard to break the mindset that had kept me close to home for most of my life, and if ever there was a time to jump ship, this was it. I felt a long way from home, and wondered why I wanted to come this far in the first place. What made me think this would be fun? These people were so strange, so foreign. Why hadn't I gone to Cuba?

I took a long nap after lunch and was asleep when I heard the drums, asleep and dreaming, trying not to think about the heat, or the Gambian men and their endless questions for the girls, or the staring children who yelled "*Tubab, tubab*" whenever I left the safety of the Friendship. Novelty had worn off, replaced by a desire for the familiar.

The shock had only been made worse by a team of tennis players who occupied the rooms above Zach and me. Every morning at five they slammed their doors in unison, banged around with their rackets, shouted indecipherable things for a few minutes, and tramped off to play tennis. I shoved my head under the covers and cursed liberally when this happened, damning them all to tennis hell for their early morning risings.

Maybe that explained why I felt so tired when the drums of the Kura Chow performance group woke me from the deep sleep of a weary man. I'd been passed out on my bed, blissfully unaware of the hard pillow or the thin mattress, oblivious to the heat and wrapped in a cocoon of air conditioning. The drums woke me, and I loathed them.

Maybe the others suffered from the same culture shock, and simply hid it better. When I stumbled blinking into the afternoon sun, I found them around a circle of drums, pounding out a beat down below. One of the performers waved me toward an open drum, and the others called for me to join them. I have the musical inclination of a bull in a china shop — all noise, no music — and had no real desire to try. But hesitantly I sat down and began to beat, my hands pounding uncertainly on the taut animal hide. I tried to make sense of the others' rhythm, but it was clear I lacked the skill to move both hands in a coordinated manner. The instructor grabbed my arms and slapped them on the drum, making every attempt more frustrating until I threw my hands up in disgust and left the others still playing their drums as I retired to the room in a sulk.

I skipped dinner, which did nothing to improve my mood, and went to bed tired and upset. Tomorrow we would head upcountry to the president's village, and I wasn't sure I wanted to go. I no longer wanted the exotic, and didn't want things to change. I longed for the familiar. I wanted to sit in my air-conditioned cocoon and ignore the world outside.

• • •

Our bus swerved wildly on the road upcountry, attempting to dodge the potholes that littered its surface. Outside, Gambians in villages paused to stare at us, watching as this bus full of strangers made its slow way through the bush.

It was hot, and I dozed. The heat seemed to be rising, growing greater the farther we strayed from the coast, and next to me I could smell Amanda's braids going bad in the sun. Small children came running up to the bus at every stop, calling *"Tubab, tubab,"* and asking for money. The sun sloped behind us, turning golden in the afternoon haze. We were on our way to Kanilai, birthplace of president Jammeh, to celebrate his birthday.

The Gambia looks like a tongue in the mouth of Senegal. That is what the Gambians say. The narrow coast belies its length as it snakes into the bush, and we'd left the familiar sights behind as we drove out of Bakau that morning. Kanilai lay somewhere on the southern bank of the Gambia River, miles inland from where we started, and we were past Yundum now, the farthest we'd ever been from the coast. The bus bumped along, the road terrible, the going slow. It had been smooth asphalt for the first hour or so, but after that it degraded quickly, and we spent most of our time on the wrong side of the road. This upcountry land was a different place than the coast, so crowded with buildings and bodies. Here spaces echoed silence, and the road was long.

Village after village crept past, accompanied by the shouts of *"Tubab"* and the sight of children waving. Occasionally we saw another vehicle, a beat-up van or truck, but mostly the road stayed empty. When Kanilai finally appeared, we welcomed the sight. The road had not been kind to my rear, or the part of me that banged continuously against the side of the bus.

A lone tank guarded the center of town, derelict and useless, and I wondered when it last ran, certain it was the only tank in the country. Tall soldiers strutted around the streets, marching by the tank and standing at attention in front of it.

On the outskirts of town sat the Sindola Lodge, its lush green contrasting sharply with the impoverished brown of the bush. White egrets strutted among water lilies in the shade of banana trees, but despite its beauty I got the feeling that the Sindola had no business when the president wasn't in town. The entire town had the look of a place with no future beyond "the home of the president," as if it would fall into disuse the moment someone overthrew him.

It wasn't long before guests began to gather outside, the colors of the ladies' dresses swirling against the shades of evening. Jammeh arrived late, dressed in his robe with his staff in hand, and his entrance caused a flurry of speeches, with officials again reminding us that Jammeh was kind enough to delay his own birthday party to celebrate the American ambassador. An army officer led everyone in a rendition of "Happy Birthday," and someone played a birthday song by a Nigerian artist. Then performers whirled and drums beat in the dark, with the tom-tom rhythm reverberating deep in my bones.

No birthday is complete without a cake, and the cooks presented Jammeh with one colored in the red, white, blue, and green stripes of the Gambian flag. His wife, a beautiful Moroccan woman the girls had taken to calling his trophy wife, stood beside him as he cut the cake, and their young daughter stood on tiptoe, peeking over the edge of the table with wide eyes.

With a politician's talent for pressing the fat, Jammeh invited everyone to shake his hand, and we lined up with the assembled Gambians to give him our best wishes. I tried to think of something clever to say, but such things rarely go over well with foreign heads of state, so I simply wished him happy birthday and shook his hand. He had a firm handshake, and his wife and daughter looked very loving, standing there beside him.

• • •

I woke the next morning to the sound of Bill pounding on the door and yelling, "It's that time!" I wanted to ignore the noise, but was once again afraid of being left behind as I pulled myself out of bed and stumbled to breakfast.

The Sindola slumbered now, the guards and debutantes gone. They had done their duty and retreated to the coast, and after our brief brush with celebrity, the morning calm was a welcome relief. The air felt cool, but the sun was warm on my chest, and it shone on the lily pads as I ate with Mary, Holly, and Sarah. We all showed the effects of a late night. The dancing and music had continued long after I went to bed, and the girls hunched over their meals, their faces reflecting the weariness I felt.

There was no rush to return to Bakau. None of us were eager to resume classes, and we had a presidential invitation to visit Kanilai's game park — a park that was part of his hometown patronage and probably didn't see many tourists this far from the coast.

A pair of dull gray rhinos greeted us at the entrance, their leathery hides shifting as they turned their heads. The sight of these creatures, idly munching grass, making a point of ignoring us and hoping we would go away, caused a stampede — though thankfully it wasn't the rhinos doing the stampeding. The human animals, on the other hand, rushed to one side of the bus and began snapping photos in a manic manner.

It made me remember the sight of Japanese tourists taking pictures of squirrels in Washington, D.C. Each one lined up, took a turn with the squirrels, and god only knows what they told their friends back home. Probably that the animals were terribly dangerous, and they were lucky to get out of there alive — exactly what I planned to tell my friends as I snapped pictures of warthogs, crocodiles, and rhinos. Never mind the bus we rode in, and the fact that the animals seemed sedated by the heat. This was Africa, and it had a certain reputation to maintain. How silly those tourists looked in Washington. How silly we looked now.

The dry grass, as high as a man, waved and rustled in faint wisps of breeze. The rump of a zebra disappeared into the grass, paying no heed as cameras clicked, and a warthog ran across the road, causing another human stampede before it vanished as well. These animals didn't concern themselves with fame. Let the animals in Tanzania and Kenya have that.

Our bus slowed at the end of the tour, curving through the bush toward a cluster of cement and wire cages. A pack of children came to follow the *tubabs*, holding our hands in silence and walking with us between compounds that held lions, ostriches, and African wild dogs. The lions peered at us, and the wild dogs twitched their saucer-like ears, looking mangy even for a species covered in calico.

We fed the ostriches, who tried to bite our fingers in gratitude. Somehow we refrained from throwing children to the lions, which looked comatose, as lions often do, and terribly out of place. All the animals had been imported, and they showed the ill effects of their displacement. This was the type of patronage that did little to benefit the Gambia, but it was a common practice. Constituents expected officials to favor their birthplace, their tribe, and their people above the country as a whole.

A lone baboon squatted in the dust near the entrance,

tied to a baobab and shuffling about at the end of his rope. His red behind showed as he paced, and other baboons scampered by, ignoring the captive and the humans boarding the bus. Kanilai disappeared behind us, its tank forgotten in the square. Weariness swept over me and I dozed again, my head lolling in the sun as the road droned on, seeming to stretch between the horizon and the sky.

When we got back it was past lunchtime. Mighty and I followed a semester student named Eric to look for food, walking down the road to a sign that read "Rhun Palm." Inside a darkened building, a crowd of young men sat in front of a small television, their eyes glued to the screen while steam poured from a kitchen at the back, and a man came out to ask what we wanted.

"You have what today?" said Eric, indicating that we each wanted a plate of whatever dish they'd prepared that afternoon.

"Chicken *yaasa*," said the man, "and rice."

A plate cost twenty-five dalasi, less than a dollar. We sat down to wait, watching the movie on the television. Men ran around an abandoned wasteland onscreen, shooting guns that made fake popping sounds when fired. The acting was amateur, like something made by high-school drama students, and I couldn't tell if it was a Gambian movie or, more likely, a product of the Nigerian film industry, third largest in the world.

When the food arrived, it appeared that chicken *yaasa* was a spicy dish of onions, lemon, and pepper. I sucked air to cool my burning tongue, eyes watering at the spicy taste, but was too hungry to stop for a few tears as we took the plates to the Friendship, eating with Bill at the bar and watching children play in the pool. The heat and dust of the road had made my throat dry, and when I asked the bar man for water, I drank half a bottle before realizing it hadn't been sealed. Until then we had only drunk from sealed bottles, provided by our hosts wherever we went, and belatedly I asked where the water came from.

"That's from the faucet," said Bill. "Didn't you know that?"

"And it's okay to drink?" My parents might have a few choice words for Bill if I died under his supervision.

"Well I drink it," he said, smiling slightly. I thought that might not mean much, since Bill had been a Peace Corps volunteer and was probably used to doing things that would make most people puke. But I grunted and drank the rest, too thirsty to care, and back in the room I told Zach I'd started drinking the water.

"I'll probably be dead by morning," I added cheerfully.

"There's blood in the water," said Zach, his eyebrows rising and falling maniacally. He laughed at my expression.

That night the excitement of the day caught up with me. I managed to stay awake until just before dinner, when the subtle call of my bed took over. Zach and I slept through the meal, and were getting ready to scrounge for scraps when we heard a knock at the door. It was Bill, carrying two plates of leftovers.

"I know how you like to eat," said Bill, grinning as he handed them over.

"Doesn't everybody?" I laughed, but he had a point. I'd been eating more and more, and the only reason they had leftovers was because I hadn't been there.

• • •

On Sunday, things changed. It was our day off, unoccupied by the lectures of the week, and we were eager for the chance to relax, to get away from it all and do something normal.

At least I was. I felt homesick, the side effect of the culture shock, and wasn't sure how to deal with it. I'd only been homesick once before, when I went away to college, and a day on the water had cured that. I'd kayaked on the river that ran past my school, enjoying the fresh air and rhythmic exercise before returning to land. There were no kayaks here, but maybe if I borrowed a wooden pirogue and went for a spin… Something about the water had a calming effect on my soul.

The problem was that every way I pictured the pirogue scenario I ended up adrift at sea, waiting for sharks to eat me before I died of dehydration. I'm not what you'd call an optimist when it comes to open boats, and hoped a day at the beach might do just as much good.

Tourists and beach bums crowded most of Bakau's beaches, along with the hawkers and hangers-on who made life tedious for those who just wanted some sun, and perhaps some solitude. There was also a class of young men offering sex to the older women, mostly Europeans, who came to the Gambia for just that reason. To avoid all this we'd been advised to visit Leybato, a beach in the nearby Fajara area that was a favorite of expats, and reputed to be quieter than most.

At breakfast I saw small leather pouches on the girls' ankles. When I asked, they said that Kawsu gave them the *ju-jus* — charms containing prayers written by an Islamic holy man called a *marabout*. Kawsu was outside now, sitting in the shade by the pool, and it took all my willpower not to jump up right then and run to get a charm of my own. I wolfed down the food as fast as I could and sprinted out, finding Kawsu yelling at children.

"Ah, Demba," he cried. "Are you all right, Demba?"

"Yes, Kawsu, I am fine!"

"Do you want your *ju-ju*, Demba? I have already given them to the girls."

I nodded eagerly, and Kawsu pulled himself to his feet, striding toward the shack where he kept the pool supplies, rummaging inside until he found a pale leather pouch the size of a matchbook. Some charms took the form of silver bracelets with scriptures written on them. Others were written out on paper, soaked in water until the ink washed off, and drunk by the person receiving the charm. This one was of the leather-and-prayers variety, and Kawsu wrapped its cord around my ankle, tightening a twist of rawhide as a cinch.

"You take it, you keep it," he said, and shook his finger at me. "You take it off only if you go in the water. It will keep you safe from evil. If a man comes at you, he cannot hurt you! Even if he comes at you in the night, with a knife," and he pantomimed a man stabbing me for good measure, "he cannot hurt you. Remember Demba," his voice echoed after me as I went to join the others. "You keep it!"

"Mistah Gilman!" said Mighty when he saw I was ready to go. We both wore our swim trunks and t-shirts, looking just like the beach bums we planned to be. Yellow taxis idled on a corner near the mosque, and Mighty stuck his head in one, dickering about the fare for a moment before he gestured for me to get in. I was still adjusting to travel in the Gambia, where the fares for regular cars and tourist taxis were always flexible, but rates for crowded vans that roared from town to town were not. I called the vans bush taxis, because I'd heard someone use the term, but "town taxi" might have been more appropriate.

The taxi dropped us by a dirt road that twisted toward the sea. Volcanic rock crumbled down into the surf, and dark figures bobbed in the water, laughing and diving wildly. I saw the girls out on the beach, absorbing the sun's rays as I ate chicken at a seaside restaurant, reflecting that I might have encountered the chicken on my way through Bakau. Chickens and goats ran around the streets, so any meal that contained either of them was guaranteed to be fresh — though sometimes you had to wait while they slaughtered the animal.

The girls looked very distracting in their bikinis. The soft hiss of waves sliding into shore soothed the tension in my muscles, and the knot that had been building in my stomach for the past few days began to loosen. I walked along the beach, footsteps falling in the sand, leaving wet impressions to be washed away by the next wave, and looked out at the sparkling horizon, enjoying the feeling of an endless panorama, as if this were eternal. The pale leather of my *ju-ju* quickly darkened with sand and wind and ocean surf, but I had already forgotten Kawsu's warning about wearing it in the water. Every so often a horse trotted by, guided by an owner who tried to get the expats to buy a ride. Gambians were consummate entrepreneurs, and dozens of people strolled along the beach selling trinkets. It was hard to resist a quick peek. Women offered massages nearby, charging a few dalasi to break some ribs in the name of relaxation, but I decided to pass and go for a swim.

The water was warm as I dove in, a welcome change from the beaches where I swam in America. They were invariably northern, blanketed in fog, and covered by water as cold as ice. This never stopped me from diving in; it just meant that when I clawed my way out again, I couldn't stop shaking for an hour. My judgment has always been spotty when it comes to the ocean.

I swam farther out, gazing up at the clear blue sky and thinking that this was just about as close to heaven as one could get. Finally, I began to feel I might have gone far enough. I'd never been the best swimmer, and my usual method involved a lot of unnecessary flailing. I'd been out of practice for years before going to the Gambia, which might explain why the shore suddenly seemed to be receding. I'd been too busy watching the girls in their bikinis to notice at first, and now the bottom had dropped out. I knew it was there somewhere, but swimming down to find it didn't seem like a good use of energy or oxygen. I started flailing, bringing back memories of happier days in my youth, when the water wasn't quite so warm, and the sun didn't shine so brightly, and I wasn't drifting out to sea.

As it turned out, flailing was also not a good use of energy or oxygen, and I tired quickly. I tried to keep my mouth above water with the backstroke, always my specialty, but I sink like a stone. All those stories you hear about people floating better in salt water are damnable lies. Every wave, even the larger ripples, sent water down my throat, often in lieu of air.

Anyone familiar with the ocean could tell you I was caught in a riptide, a current capable of pulling even the strongest swimmer out to sea. Small wonder it had no trouble with me. I had a good idea it was a riptide, because my guidebook warned about avoiding them, though it failed to mention what to do once caught. Swimming directly in, as I tried to do, exhausts a swimmer without freeing him from the current. The correct technique is to swim parallel to the shore until free of the riptide, and then proceed leisurely in. That might have been handy information to include.

Every glance I stole at the shoreline showed it to be a receding one. I began to consider the odds of drifting out to sea and waiting for a passing boat to find me — the odds didn't look good — when I noticed Debbie and Eric nearby. I gasped out a cry for help, then another and another until I felt them grab hold. Together they dragged me in to shore, their hands under my arms as they hauled me up the beach, and I lay on my towel, alternately gasping for air and coughing up seawater. I had never felt so tired in my life.

My feet dragged in the sand on the walk back to the Friendship. We'd decided not to take a taxi, and my limbs felt leaden, the weariness making the walk longer than it really was. I spent most of the afternoon in bed, but that night I climbed out the window and over the air conditioner to talk to my family, waiting on the balcony until they rang up on Bill's cell phone. It was strange to think I was talking to them from Africa, overlooking an empty court-yard as I wished my brother happy birthday from four thousand miles away. He told me he wanted a *ju-ju* for a birthday present. My parents were just glad to hear I was alive, still sure that Africa would kill me. I didn't tell them about the riptide.

## Chapter Seven
# Caged Hyenas

For a man who spent the previous day almost drowning, I woke up eager to face a new dawn. Had we only been here a week? The ups and downs of the last few days made it seem longer, but I felt ready to go, as if the beach had cleared my senses, made me see things in a new light.

Our second Monday in country found us in class again, seated in the sweltering room and trying to learn about Gambian time. They measure it in large blocks, based on the Muslim prayer times that set the rhythm of daily life, but the most important thing was that Gambians were never on time. They operated on Gambia Maybe Time: maybe they would show up, or maybe not, and they liked to point out that it was only natural for them to follow GMT — as they're also on Greenwich Mean Time — then smile in a self-satisfied way as if they had just made the world's greatest pun.

This was something that we, as college students, loved. Things happened slowly, or not at all, and as if to drive the point home, our scheduled guests failed to appear at lunch, and then again at dinner, leaving me wondering how many times we would find ourselves waiting on Gambians determined to observe their own version of the clock.

We rose at seven the next morning, denying my body the breakfast it deserved as we practiced for our trip upcountry. At the end of the week we would travel away from the coast, beginning on the river's north bank, and we'd have to get up early to catch the first ferry out of Banjul. I'd assumed a bridge would span the wide river, which divided the Gambia and Senegal, but I was wrong.

"It's a long wait if you miss the first ferry," warned Bill, and we believed him. There was no such thing as a short wait in the Gambia.

If you looked at the country from the air, you'd see concrete extended along the marshlands of the coast, and a small divot of green knocked out of the gray — Abuko Nature Reserve, where we drove after missing breakfast, five miles from Bakau on the edge of the sprawl near Yundum. Craig Emms, a pale-haired Brit who worked with the trust that ran Abuko, was happy to talk to us in Darwin Field Station, a small hut almost hidden in trees by the banks of a pond, where lily pads floated on still water. Across the pond, a deer-like marshbuck stood stiffly, twitching its ears and braving the banks despite Craig's claim of crocodiles in the water. An equally brave kingfisher dove from a tree, darting across the water and snapping a meal with barely a ripple before he returned to the tree and began eating contentedly.

I was used to hearing about the loss of biodiversity when species are confined to smaller and smaller habitats. Given its size, Abuko didn't lack for species, and the park seemed like the Gambia, with a little bit of everything in a tiny package. It boasted one hundred fifteen types of plants, two hundred fifty kinds of birds, thirty-seven reptiles, fifty-two mammal species — not counting humans — and showed the potential of the Gambian environment if managed properly.

Melang, a short Gambian with a goatee, showed us around the reserve, pointing out different species so we could promptly forget their names. A monkey watched from the trees, sitting on a branch like a sagacious old man with his red face turned toward us, and his brethren scampered among fallen branches and roots in the brush, pausing to stare with dark eyes. Ahead of us a line of black crossed the path, shifting over the pale dirt, and closer inspection revealed a train of ants. The tiny creatures scuttled back and forth among the leaves, their mission unknown to us but clear to them.

"Do not disturb them," cautioned Melang. "If you step in their way they will attack you."

After seeing the way the monkeys moved in freedom, it was sad to see how they looked in captivity. Guinea baboons paced in a chain-link pen at the end of the tour, with a ladder and a few rope swings for exercise. They seemed resigned to sit and stare out at their captors, near another cage that held spotted hyenas. The hyenas paced and stared too, looking slightly less than bloodthirsty and avoiding the heckling laughter that makes them sound almost human in the bush.

"They can mimic human voices," said Isaac, whispering the secret as if the hyenas would jump out if he said it too loud. "When they hear your name, they'll start mimicking the sound. You'll hear someone calling your name in the dark and it'll be hyenas." I shuddered, and decided not to wander off into the bush if I ever heard someone calling my name at night.

A tawny male lion sat in a third enclosure, growling and chewing on a red haunch of meat, shaking his mane and tearing the oversized steak apart, his great paws holding it as he gnawed. The girls winced and the vegetarians in the group cringed at the sight, but my stomach growled. I licked my lips as the lion ate, reminded of the missed breakfast that morning.

"I'm jealous," I said. "Where's my steak?" But I felt better now that we were in the open air, away from the stuffy classroom. The past few days had seen a change in my outlook, and I was sure that food had something to do with it. I'd always been a picky eater, from the days as a kid when I hid uneaten green beans in my napkin, to the days at college when I sprinted past the green beans toward the fried chicken. The Gambia challenged me, and I'd spent the first few days staring at plates of hot, inedible food — inedible to me, anyway. This is never a good way to improve one's temper, but the experience at the beach had shocked me, jolting me out of my reluctance to try new things. I suppose I was grateful, because it made me look at the world with fresh eyes, reminding me life was too short to spend complaining.

• • •

Due east of Abuko, the bus drove down a dirt road and stopped in a ramshackle collection of whitewashed huts, where a band of water shimmered between green mangrove trees and I could smell the sea. Oyster shells lay everywhere, and hand-painted signs covered a baobab, advertising tours, taxi drivers, and "the best guide." It seemed like a wonderful idea: a billboard as lovely as a tree. Pirogues floated in the dark water, some carved from a single tree and filled with nets and lines, their sides worn smooth by the hands of their owners. Others were elegant things with shaded platforms, meant more for tourists than fish, and a few sailboats floated farther out, modern boats built in some shipyard and sailed into the deeper channels by Westerners.

Oysters lived on the roots of mangroves that crowded the channel, and village women harvested them, burning the shells to make lime and whitewash. A causeway led into the swamp, half packed earth and half rough planks above shells glinting in the water below, and the planks bounced under our feet on the way to Lamin Lodge, a shack that stuck out of the mangroves. We sat in the shade and sipped cool sodas, gazing out at the pale blue sky and watching the boats move slowly on the water.

Green monkeys clambered up to greet us, peering over the walls and posing for pictures, hopping around as if quite accustomed to human visitors. One took the soda I'd been drinking and clasped the bottle in his tiny paws, tipping it back and sipping greedily at the sweet liquid. The rest followed suit with the girls' drinks, pausing and looking up at us as if to say "What?" Later I realized that we shouldn't have been so quick to give the monkeys our drinks — soda is no better for monkeys than it is for humans, and if the animals get too much sugar in their diet they can develop diabetes — but there wasn't a sign saying "Don't feed the animals," so we did what tourists do when there's no sign — we fed the animals.

At lunchtime we drove to Gambia College, part of the University of the Gambia. Flame trees dotted the campus, their spreading branches lit by brilliant orange blossoms, but the blossoms were the only color in the scene. The rest was drab, the rooms bare, the lab equipment broken, the blackboards cracked, and when we took part in a discussion about AIDS in the auditorium, the room echoed hollowly. As we ate with the students they asked us about America, and I wondered what it would be like to go to college in a place like this. Across the table, Zach fussed at me as I sipped gingerly at a soda, unable to drink much because of the spicy rice in my stomach.

"You're going to get dehydrated, Andrew," he said. "Drink!"

• • •

When not confined to class or allowed to wander the streets, I got more than my share of second-hand smoke from Abby and Christina, who took frequent smoking breaks on the walks overlooking the pool.

"I'm trying to quit," said Abby, and took a drag.

"So am I," said Christina, also taking a drag.

Outside the hotel gates, men sold cigarettes in packs or one at a time, making it that much harder to quit. When the girls bought single cigarettes, sold by a man who always had a lighter handy, it was easy enough to say "just one more" and not have to deal with an entire pack.

When I wasn't trying to catch cancer via second-hand smoke, Zach and I retreated to the air-conditioned comfort of our room. I'd recovered somewhat from my bad mood the week before, but still wasn't ready to spend every moment outside. I needed that cocoon for as long as it would hold. The power went out frequently, leaving us comatose in darkness, sometimes for half an hour, sometimes all night long, but when I looked out the window I could see electric lights shining all around us.

"Why does everyone have power except us?" I complained to Zach the third or fourth time this happened. I didn't really expect an answer, but I wanted to voice my frustrations.

"They all have generators," said Zach.

"You think everyone has a generator and they all switch on the second the power goes off? Then why don't we?"

Even when the power stayed on, the light in the bathroom had the disconcerting habit of burning out, leaving us in darkness, trying to use the toilet or take a shower blind. The shower, when it worked, came on cold and stayed that way, which was greatly appreciated in the hot sun but less so in cold air-conditioning. Mighty ran in and out, fixing the bathroom light or just sitting and talking, grinning at us when we asked about the Gambia. We weren't particularly eager to spend time outside of our small group, still adjusting to life in a strange place, and we stuck close to home, but we couldn't take the Friendship's peace for granted. A slender girl named Ami stopped by every day to bang on our door and ask if she could clean the room. Zach and I let her, because the amount of sand we tracked in could have made its own beach, but we quickly learned to weigh our options when she arrived.

"Do you have any pens for me?" she asked every time we opened the door. Whoever first decided to hand out pens to the children of the world, I hope they feel good about it. I'm sure the intention was pure, but travelers have been paying for it ever since, greeted with outstretched hands of want instead of outstretched hands of greeting.

Neither Zach nor I had pens to give, but Ami hung about anyway, asking if she could have our things and ignoring subtle hints to leave. We took to hiding in the room and locking the door, hoping she hadn't seen us go in. If she had, she would wait outside for half an hour, pounding on the door and shouting our names in a singsong voice.

Aside from that, daily life settled into a comfortable routine. Bill still offered to find us a room with the others, but the girls complained of being eaten alive by mosquitoes, kept awake at night by their whining drone, and we'd discovered an unexpected benefit to living one story up. The bugs rarely made it that high, and the nets above our beds remained curled and unused, just another reminder that we were in a foreign place.

We still ate our meals in the dining hall, where we were usually the only diners. I'd begun to appreciate Gambian cooking, when it didn't set my mouth on fire, and lunch and dinner were always delicious: chicken or freshly caught fish, a peanut stew called *domoda*, rice and beans and vegetables. It was simple food, but it filled us up.

Our usual breakfast, on the other hand, consisted of bread, fried eggs and Tang, and I soon stopped trying to eat in the morning. It was easier to roll out of bed right before class and stumble down to the lecture room. This did little to improve my early morning moods, but I felt better rested the day after our trip to Abuko, when we had to study verbs in Mandinka. Conjugating strange words has never been my strong suit, and I learned almost nothing from the lesson. Frustration began to grow again, and I was glad when we moved to the cultural lesson on marriage in the Gambia, where the law allowed a man up to four wives.

"What do you *mean* they can have multiple wives?" demanded Casey, sputtering a bit. "How can the women *stand* it?"

"It is very difficult sometimes," said Bakary, "if the wives do not like each other. But it is also difficult for the husband! He must be careful to treat them fairly, so that he does not anger one wife. Otherwise he will not be happy!"

This did little to placate the girls, who looked ready to start a revolt.

"You know, we had polygamy before Islam in the Gambia," Bakary went on. "We used to have more than just four. But it says in the Koran that if a man can afford it, he may have up to four wives. So when the Muslims came and said 'You can keep polygamy, but only four wives,' people agreed. But when the Christians came and said 'You can't do that, that is not right. Only one man, one woman...' nobody wanted to listen!"

In the Bakau market after lunch, University of the Gambia students led us in a mapping exercise to hone our anthropological skills. We came into the market through the back, where the stench of rotting fish filled the air and the desiccated brown things lay on wood tables with their eyes rotted out, hidden under a haze of flies. It took us half an hour to canvas the area, in spite of Yaukuba, a student who appointed himself the leader of our expedition and delighted in barking out orders that no one obeyed. We walked from stall to stall, noting the location of fishmongers, fruit vendors, shops selling bootleg videos, and a wizened cobbler who sat cross-legged by the road, his tools spread in front of him, scattered among old leather shoes and worn-out soles. In the Bakau craft market, shops displayed silver and brightly colored cloth, and curious shopkeepers poked their heads out to see what we were doing.

"Oh, you are with the university," cried one woman when we explained our task. "That is where my child goes!" She scooped up some trinkets and pressed them into our hands, beaming as we thanked her and waved goodbye, our notebooks still out, scribbling furiously.

The other shopkeepers clamored for attention, their voices given a desperate edge by the end of the tourist season, and every time we stopped men gathered around the girls, asking if they had Gambian husbands. Hawkers pulled out necklaces, trying to sell things that were on sale in every shop, things we were trying to resist. Soon the constant parade of bright colors and wild patterns was too much, and our footsteps slowed until we stopped in front of a stall with a cow horn on display.

"How are you, my brother?" called the woman inside, coming out to greet me. "How is the day?" Gambians always asked about "the day" and never "your day."

"The day is good."

"You want cowrie shell?"

"No, not today. How much is the cow horn?"

"One hundred," said the woman without batting an eye. She'd probably found the thing lying in the street and put it out on display, but I was suddenly seized with the urge to buy it.

"One hundred? No, how about sixty."

"Sixty is too little, my brother. You pay eighty."

I scratched my chin and agreed, and as she pocketed the money, I realized I had no idea what to do with a cow horn. Maybe fend off the hawkers on my way back to the Friendship.

• • •

The next day we learned how to take a taxi in Mandinka.

This was something I never planned to do. I knew if I tried, I would end up in Senegal without even knowing it. The only sign would be that suddenly, no one spoke English anymore.

Weariness got the better of me as the afternoon heat descended, and I crept up to my room, too tired for another session with the university students. Still suffering the lingering effects of culture shock, I was in the room when Zach returned from class.

"You lazy bastard," he said, seeing me hunched over his computer. We were friends by now, and a little profanity between us was nothing, so I told him to cram a sock in it.

"Are you even going to the drumming?" The Kura Chow group was back for a second performance.

"That didn't go so well last time," I said, thinking that nobody needed a reminder of my musical abilities. I stayed in the room until dinner, listening to the drums outside, and emerged to find the sun setting across the sky, streaking the clouds with gold.

I was in a better mood the following morning. The struggle to learn the language of this new culture, to obey every custom — the struggle to assimilate — had been the biggest reason for my culture shock and retreat into the room. Struggling to fit in, and trying to be someone I wasn't, only wore me down. Now I realized there was no way I was ever going to be a Gambian. It was impossible, after all, and the realization that I would never adjust completely, that in the end it was someone else's world, eased the pressure. If I wasn't going to try and be a Gambian, who was I going to be? I didn't know, but I looked forward to finding out.

In our cross-cultural discussion that day, we made lists of American superstitions, telling the Gambians about shamrocks, black cats, broken mirrors, lucky socks, and walking under ladders.

"It's bad luck if the groom sees the bride in her dress before the wedding," we told the Gambians, who began to look at us strangely.

"But good luck if they have 'something old, something new, something borrowed, something blue,'" added Abby. The Gambians looked at us as if we'd gone mad, but we laughed at the list we made, poking fun at our own traditions. As strange as Gambian culture might seem at times, it probably wasn't any weirder than our own once we took a step back. When the session ended, Bakary's hands shook as he gave me papers he'd written on crafts in the Gambia, the pages of the documents old and stained between his wrinkled fingers.

"I will find my proposal on museums and bring it to you," he promised as he left. I took the papers to my room, and fell asleep until a rumbling in my stomach roused me long enough to wolf down dinner. When I went back to sleep I felt different, as if a weight had been lifted from my chest. The *ju-ju* had improved my spirits, the beach did a bit more, and Abuko was even better, but the real difference was internal. I began to look with curiosity rather than annoyance at the new world around me. Instead of something to fight against, it became something to be enjoyed. There was still very little privacy — there is almost never privacy in Africa — and I was still tired of the constant presence of strangers, but I felt myself coming out of a shell. I went to sleep happy, realizing I could just be myself in this strange land, aided in this sudden satisfaction by the knowledge that we were driving south to the ocean tomorrow. There is nothing like the prospect of a day at the beach to buoy one's spirits. I just hoped I wouldn't drown.

## Chapter Eight
# Beachcombing

The road ran south, straight and black in the sun, and we drove along the coast as it stretched from village to village toward Casamance, an oft-rebellious region of Senegal that kept trying to break away from the rest of the country. The bush raced past, the long train of rusty green broken only occasionally by human habitation, and I breathed deep, enjoying our release from the crowded confines of Bakau.

I'd paid little attention on our last day of classes, wishing I were outside where children splashed in the pool, seeking relief while leggy figures ran back and forth on the hotel tennis courts. Our session on socializing was equally dull, even when our professors talked about the ritual of *ataaya*, the dark tea served in Senegal and the Gambia as a social drink. I longed to actually encounter these things, instead of talking about them in some stuffy lecture hall.

We'd left Bakau that afternoon, heading along the coastal road, peering around with the eager air of seagoing beachcombers, and after an hour we turned off the asphalt and bumped down a dirt road, smelling smoke before we saw huts clustered by the sea and racks of fish drying in the sun.

"This is Gunjur," said Bill as he hopped out. Men and women pressed in at the open windows, pushing fish at us. "We don't want your fish," we said, but it seemed unthinkable to the villagers that persistence wouldn't win us over. They pushed the fish farther in, shocked that we didn't want the smelly things. The men in particular refused to give up, eying the girls with obvious interest, their hands everywhere until I remembered what Bill told me about crime in the Gambia.

"There's very little, and it's mostly petty theft, scams, pickpocketing," he had said, and then paused. "But you have to remember, a lot of these people are desperate. Things happen."

I suspected that the things he meant might have more impact on women than men. Women have it considerably harder in the Gambia, a fact that became clear whenever we left the hotel grounds. Gambians expect a girl to refuse advances, even when she's interested, and Gambian men had not yet learned that "no means no."

The misunderstanding rarely resulted in violence, but one of girls had already been offered money for sex. Men propositioned all of them, for sex, for marriage, for general "relations," but only one was offered money. Zach and I were in the lobby when she came in, distraught and almost in tears, and we stood awkwardly, unsure how to respond as the girls comforted their own, feeling slightly offended by our gender. But when we left, I looked at Zach and wondered how much the man had offered.

"Not enough, I guess," laughed Zach, and suddenly it didn't seem like just Gambians who were insensitive.

Now the Gunjur men pushed in at the windows, and flies filled the air, landing on the fish and crawling on our skin. Small children called for money when we left the vehicles, clinging to our arms and trying to put hands in pockets that didn't belong to them. Acrid gray rose from fires under racks of fish, and the stench hung thickly over shacks and a fleet of pirogues that rode just offshore, floating lightly at anchor beyond the breaking waves. Bow and stern anchors held the boats lengthwise to the waves, making them rock back and forth in time with the rolling sea, displaying the painted sides that made each a work of art.

Gulls wheeled overhead and dogs ran about the beach, sniffing at fish carcasses or biting the occasional crab that scuttled frantically across the sand. We could see the curve of the bay in the distance, and left the persistent men and children behind, our footsteps falling in long lines toward the headland, making clear impressions in the wet sand. The crowd thinned, leaving us with quiet. Out here the sun seemed to shine more brightly, the sky unblemished by clouds or smoking fires. Gunjur looked more picturesque from across the bay, its smell blown inland and its men retreating to wait for our return. Palm trees waved, their fronds tossing and rustling above the bushes dotting the headland. Volcanic outcroppings jutted into the sea, sharp and broken as we waded in the shallows, picking our way between the red stone where hermit crabs scuttled, their shells ranging from dark brown to pale yellow.

With some reluctance we turned back, unwilling to rejoin the crowd and leave this seclusion behind. A boat was putting out to sea when we returned, its bow pointed toward the horizon and its sides swept by charging surf as a thin man balanced on the prow, leaning jauntily and guiding the boat with a long pole. He kept the bow into the waves as another man pushed at the stern, his bright red trousers trailing in the surf. Surrounded by a rainbow of colors, block letters on the side proclaimed the boat "Cheikh," the king of the seas.

"Do you want to see them making cashew wine?" Bill asked as we drove away from Gunjur. I'd noticed the swollen fruits hanging in the trees, ripe and yellow with the large shell of the cashew nut protruding from the bottom. The shell contained a caustic acid that would burst out and burn the skin if handled improperly. Caution was needed when harvesting the nut, but Bill's question seemed unnecessary. Of course we wanted to see them making cashew wine.

In the shade of a cashew tree by the roadside, two women hunched over a trough made from a tree trunk, their muscular shoulders and arms bare. Rhythmically they pressed the fruit down in the trough, letting the juice run out the bottom into a plastic bucket, surrounded by discarded fruit and buckets already filled with frothy yellow juice. Both women looked up, their strong hands squeezing out more juice. One of them took a pestle and pounded it up and down on the fresh fruits, crushing them into a pulp, but the other just smiled and kept pressing, her red cheeks gleaming.

Looking for the end result of their labor, we drove down another dirt road, our tires hitting hard ruts, until we arrived at a cluster of huts in a mango grove. At the sound of slamming car doors, an elderly man hobbled out from under a thatched roof, bent over a gnarled walking stick, and a group of children gathered to stare at the white people. The elderly patron greeted Bill as the children hung back and watched the *tubabs* in their midst. We stared back, eying the mud brick and woven reed of their house, with its thatched roof and darkened interior, until the old man said something to his brood and a young boy ran inside.

The family was Christian, free from paying even lip service to rules that might prevent a Muslim from making alcohol, and the boy returned quickly, carrying two old bottles, one filled with opaque cashew wine, the other with a clear liquid. We tried the "wine" first, the yellow liquid thick with pulp. Up to that point, I had never been a drinker. It wasn't that I'd never had alcohol, but half a Jell-O shot is hardly a proper introduction. Cashew wine made a very pleasant introduction, if not a refined one. I took another sip and smacked my lips before passing it down the line.

"They call this local stuff 'zoom-zoom,'" said Bill, handing me the second bottle, the one with the clear liquid. "It's got quite a kick to it."

"What the hell," I thought, and took a sip.

My belly burned. My throat felt like fire. Sweat poured from my brow. I coughed violently, and took another sip. Here was something you wouldn't find in America, not unless you went up into the backwoods and looked for moonshine. Unlike its sweet cousin, cashew rum introduced itself like a prizefighter — with a hard right. To the best of my knowledge I've never made a habit of drinking cleaning fluid, but that came close, and I recommend it for anyone who has no taste buds and wants to risk blindness. I coughed again and passed the bottle, watching as the others eyed the zoom-zoom greedily, leaving doubts that we could trust anyone with its safe passage back to the Friendship.

"Give it to Andrew," suggested Bill, who knew that I'd once been a teetotaler. "He'll look after it, right?"

"Sure, Bill," I said, grabbing the bottle and clutching it to my chest, already beginning to doubt my ability to keep it safe. Something broke inside me when I drank that cashew rum — probably my esophagus, since the stuff burned with a fiery passion — and I enjoyed it. After that, I would drink anything anyone put in front of me.

• • •

With our alcohol bought, the family waved goodbye and the huts faded in the trees behind us. We drove away until the ocean appeared, growing larger as we crested a ridge and it came fully into view, the surf breaking on the soft gray sand of Sanyang beach.

The beach shared its name with Kukoi Samba Sanyang, the man who led the 1981 coup attempt against president Jawara. Sanyang had made an effort to join the government by other means, twice seeking election to Parliament, but by 1981 he decided that enough was enough. Personally, I would have written a stern letter to the editor, but Sanyang tried to take over the government while Jawara was away in London, and a week of bloodshed left several hundred dead before Senegalese troops intervened to put down the rebels.

Suffused with brotherly love over the spilling of blood, the two countries signed a treaty the following year and became the Senegambia Confederation — the closest they would ever be to a single country. The goal was to combine their armed forces and economies, but some things just don't work out, and the Gambia withdrew from the Confederation in 1989.

"In Senegal we like to say that the Gambia has 'peace and peanuts,'" said one of our speakers, and began to tell us how Gambians chose to remain independent from Senegal because they didn't trust the Senegalese. The way he talked about the Gambia and Senegal, they sounded like two friendly neighbors, joshing each other and occasionally quarreling over whose dog shit on the other's lawn.

Bill and the rest dove into the sea at Sanyang, splashing and bodysurfing the bigger waves. Only Amy, a graduate student doing research in the Gambia, stayed on shore with me, and I left her guarding our bags and wandered off. I had my reasons for not diving in. Memories of the riptide at Leybato still lingered. It had shaken me, and the adrenaline of struggling against the ocean made me realize there were bigger things to fear than just the strangeness of a new place. Even if I wasn't afraid of the water, I was painfully aware of my own mortality and my status as an infinitesimal speck in the great vast ocean.

The sun shone faintly, hidden behind a pale haze as the last fading remnants of the *harmattan*, the desert wind that blows off the Sahara every year, swirled westward through the atmosphere. As I walked the beach, searching for shells, I became aware that someone had joined me, and looked up to see a skinny man in a t-shirt and shorts watching me.

"I am Steve Baba," he said. "You are a tourist?"

"No," I said, used to Gambians asking me this. It was one part of being a white traveler in Africa, the immediate identification as an outsider. For obvious reasons, no one bothered to ask if I was from the area. My skin instantly set me apart from Gambians, making it difficult to get the "good price" or avoid demands for money. I thought that was what Steve wanted, and turned away.

"You are not a tourist?" he said, following after me. "You come here why?"

"To study."

"I like Bob Marley," he said, his footsteps falling next to mine. "One love!"

"Yes, one love," I smiled, finding his enthusiasm hard to ignore. "I like Bob Marley too."

"Different colors, one people," he sang, repeating lyrics I heard more than once in the Gambia. "Different colors… one people… It's good!"

"Yes, it's good," I said, pacing and combing the strand. Away from the tourists the beach hadn't been picked clean, and I paused as Steve rambled, stooping to pick up a spiral shell or broken sand dollar.

"You like the shells?" said Steve. "You want conch? I will bring you conch." He ran off and came back holding two small conch shells. "I give you good price."

"No, no, it's okay," I said. I didn't want to buy any shells. I wanted to find my own.

"You don't want conch?"

"No, I don't want conch." I stopped to pick up a cowrie shell, hoping for the good luck that Gambians believed it would bring. Steve tossed the conch aside, running off and coming back with more shells. He pushed a beautiful spiral at me, and I told him that really, it was too much. I didn't want to buy anything.

"No, here," he said, pressing it into my hand. "It is a gift." I stuck the shell in my pocket, and Steve looked out where the others played in the ocean.

"Can you talk to the girls for me?" he asked, wanting a wingman. "Maybe they need Gambian boyfriend?"

"Oh," I said, feigning chagrin, "they are all married." The girls always told would-be suitors that their husbands were waiting for them back at the hotel or just up ahead, and always said their husbands were big, jealous fellows who wouldn't tolerate any nonsense on the side.

Steve's face fell. "Even the fat one?" he said, and nodded toward Amy, sitting by herself among our bags.

"Yes, even the fat one."

I stopped to examine a stranded Portuguese man-of-war, its pink and purple sail still inflated, examining the deadly tentacles trailing in the sand. Steve and I walked back and forth, one of us trying to find solitude, the other following behind. He was friendly — too friendly — asking questions about America and the girls when all I really wanted was to wander, looking for shells in the sand.

Finally, the others left the water. I pressed fifty dalasi into Steve's hand, gathered my things and went to the van, joined by cattle that walked slowly past, placidly regarding the world and ignoring the *tubabs* among them, followed by herders who walked with switches balanced on their shoulders, ready to swat the rumps of vagrant cows.

I grew sleepy as we rode north, passing the houses and fish shacks and a bright orange arch that stood near the village of Tanje, marking the entrance to Tanje Village Museum.

"They've got a couple of blacksmiths and a weaver there," said Bill. "And they have rooms, if you want to stay for a few days and study with the blacksmiths."

I was still considering working with blacksmiths, and I mulled Bill's offer as we roared north, wondering if I was willing to stay by myself, away from the protective shelter of my fellow Americans. In two days we would leave the comfort of the Friendship, journeying upcountry for a week. None of us were sure what we'd find, and after that we would set our own paths for the last four weeks of the field school. Until then we were still together, and the laughter of the others kept too many thoughts of the future at bay.

## CHAPTER NINE
# Away from the Coast

Two weeks in, the first part of our journey ended. With language and culture classes complete, it was time to travel upcountry. So far we hadn't ventured far from paved roads, the safety of flush toilets, and the comforting glow of electric lights. The farthest we'd been was Kanilai, but soon the ocean breezes would be a distant whisper.

We planned to leave the hotel at dawn, but the best-laid plans fall apart in Africa, and with the vagaries of last-minute packing it wasn't until nine that we left the hotel to catch the ferry from Banjul. To our chagrin we arrived too late to catch the ten o'clock boat, and found our van transformed into an oven as we waited for the next one and hawkers surrounded us, pushing their wares in the windows. Beyond the ferry dock the gray-green river surged toward the sea, close enough that the smell of salt water permeated the air, accompanied by pungent whiffs of fish and open sewers. So near to the ocean itself, the river looked endless, the other side hidden in a distant haze.

Gradually an iron monster hove into view, moving closer and closer until we could make it out — first the boxy shape of the ferry itself, then the vehicles on its lower deck, and finally the figures standing on the upper deck, waiting as the behemoth docked, disgorging cars coughing blue smoke, Gambians, and Senegalese.

The ferry was of the type generally reserved for shipwrecks. I'd heard about an incident where a sister ship stalled and drifted out to sea, and as the ferry pulled away from the dock, beginning the long slow crawl across the gray expanse, I prayed the old girl had enough in her to reach the north bank.

Rotting stumps of old pilings dotted the shore, their black tops disappearing under the slow swell of waves rolling in. I left the breathless confines of the van to climb to the ferry's top deck, already crowded with passengers, and from my iron perch I could just make out the haze of the far bank. With no wind to offer relief, the slow rocking of the boat and the intense heat soon reduced me to watching the shore inch closer, the press of the other passengers only exacerbating the heat and making me ill.

The Gambia River is less than three miles wide where it funnels between Banjul and Barra point, but the ferry crept along at a snail's pace. It swayed to one side, lazily riding the waves sliding into the harbor, and I checked the far shore. It didn't seem to be getting any closer. The boat swayed the other way. This was faster than swimming, but not by much. The rhythm seemed to go on forever. I'd never been seasick in my life, but the tedium and the sun overhead made the otherwise gentle rocking almost unbearable as my stomach echoed the rolling motion. The sweltering air suffocated me, making my head droop with exaggerated weariness.

I didn't throw up, which was fortunate for the people below, but it was a serious temptation. The rolling made me think the ferry might decide to turn clean over, then drift out to sea with us scraping along the bottom. I was grateful for the small mercy that it didn't, and even more grateful when the shore came closer, and then closer still, until finally we were off the boat and could exchange the monotony and heat of the waves for the monotony and heat of a long drive in the bush.

Our first stop was Fort Bullen, a ruin built by the British in their days as colonial masters of the Gambia. The British used the fort, now a United Nations heritage site, to enforce the end of the slave trade, and manned it in World War II to defend the colony against a Senegal controlled by Vichy France.

Children greeted us when we arrived, balancing platters of bright mangoes on their heads. Colonial cannons and guns from World Wars littered the crumbling fort, guarded by yellow and blue agama lizards that darted away from our approach, watching from the corner of their eyes and pumping their front legs until we nicknamed them "push-up" lizards. Scraggly cacti surrounded the fort, and the guide plucked a few of their red fruits, showing us how to reach the sweetness inside. It was delicious, but I spent the rest of the day trying to extract cactus spines from my fingers.

From Fort Bullen we headed toward Juffreh-Albreda. This small village might have existed in complete obscurity if Alex Haley never wrote *Roots*, the chronicle of his ancestor Kunta Kinte, taken from his home of Juffreh and sold into slavery in America. Despite some doubts about the story's basis, Haley apparently believed it, and both the Gambian government and Juffreh locals seized on the story as a way of gaining money and prestige. The villagers gladly relate Kunta Kinte's tale to any who take the time to listen, and every other year the Gambia hosts a Roots festival, hoping to attract emigrated Africans and their money back to their own roots.

As soon as we drove away from Fort Bullen and into Niumi, we entered another Africa. Not the Western-style hotel or even the "tourist safari" Africa offered by game parks. It was as if we crossed an invisible line in the cracked dirt and found ourselves in a land of thatched mud huts and cattle. This was what I'd dreamed of since I first saw *Tubabs in Africa*, a glimpse of a faraway land, something I'd never seen before. Surely, life would be strange here.

It was hard to imagine Niumi once holding sway over the rest of the region, extracting tribute from the north and south banks. There was none of that faded glory in the dusty plains. Now the north bank is neglected, unpowered and cut off from the south, with roads that slowed us to a crawl and threatened to tenderize us before we ever made it to our first night's rest.

"If you think these roads are bad," said Bill, "wait till you see the south bank."

Skirting the river's course, we drove through swamps and marshes, past olive-green water lying still among bushes half-submerged below the opaque surface. Thorny trees clung to the edge, and beyond them stood tall palms, their trunks straight as arrows.

I experienced a mild culture shock relapse upcountry. Fewer and fewer people spoke English, and amenities like air conditioning, clean drinking water, and electricity all but disappeared. Heading into the interior, I felt as though we were traveling into the proverbial heart of darkness, and realized I'm given to using terrible clichés.

Deep pink flowers greeted us on the river's edge in Albreda, a village founded by a Wolof man named Musa Gaye and used for years as a French trading post before they ceded control to the British. Like the man who made my *juju*, the founder of the village was a *marabout*, a holy man who combined the traditional beliefs of West Africa and the newer, imported beliefs of Muslim conquerors.

In the middle of the river the crumbling ruins of Fort James clung to the top of James Island, a dark lump in the surging water we walked down to, waiting for a boat to take us to the island while villagers gathered around. Some stared silently, others asked for money or pens. Debbie struck up a conversation in Mandinka, but I hung back, having already forgotten my lessons and tired of being gawked at.

Up close the water looked olive green, dull and sickly, and the skeletal frames of shrimp traps bobbed around us when the boat arrived to take us out, with the fishermen tending them balanced on narrow pirogues. Even miles from the coast, salt water splashed my face as waves smacked the sides of our boat. Slow and wide, the Gambia River never raced, but gave the impression it wouldn't let anything stand in its way.

The island drew closer, stark against the sky, ruins crowning a dry hill and barren trees clawing at the air with twisting branches. It was smaller than I expected, a single craggy spur, the edges collapsing in the endless current. Originally built by the Germans, then held by the Dutch until the English captured it, the fort and its island changed hands between the French and English several times over the next century. Situated on the artery of the Gambia River, it served as a collection point for slaves until the British abolished the trade in their colonial dominions. After that, the fort enforced the abolition of the trade it had once supported, and a "freedom pole" looked out at the lonely island from shore. The story went that if a slave escaped from Fort James, swam to shore, and touched the pole, he would be set free — no small feat, considering the current and the distance.

We clambered about when we reached the island, walking among broken walls and the gaping maws of empty cannons. "Move along now," the cannons seemed to say, pointing out at the gray water where two fishermen in a tiny canoe rowed across the sunset. From the island's crown I could make out the river's far shore, a dim shadow easily mistaken for a trick of the light, and I peered at it for a moment, trying to discern its secrets before going down to find the boat waiting. As the pirogue's prow cut toward shore, I glanced back over my shoulder. The island looked forlorn, shrinking in the distance, a crumbling monument to a bygone age, forgotten by its colonial masters and left alone in the river.

I walked back to the hotel with a young student named Boubacar, one of many Boubacars we met, distinguished from the others when the girls called him their Gambian husband.

"How do you find the Gambia?" he asked as we walked, our footsteps almost the only sound in the village.

"It's very nice," I said, and asked him what he thought of President Jammeh. These were the two questions we exchanged with Gambians who, if they weren't satisfied with our assessment of their country, put us on the spot by asking if we liked America or the Gambia better — a comparison I didn't feel qualified to make.

Boubacar pondered the question a moment. "I think he is okay. He does not like journalists, and maybe he has not done as much as he said he would, but he is better than Jawara."

It was an opinion I heard many times — that in spite of his faults (a bit of nepotism, a penchant for throwing journalists in prison, and a habit of promising more than he could deliver), Jammeh was a welcome relief from the tedium of Jawara's reign. But would they feel the same way in ten years, if Jammeh kept holding on to power?

"We will see," said Boubacar, and shrugged in the indefatigable Gambian manner, his hands raised a bit as if to add, "What can you do?"

I whiled away the remaining daylight in a hammock at the hotel, watching beautiful birds fly in and out of the trees above me, listening to their song until dusk fell. When darkness closed in I noticed a change from the ready brilliance of the Friendship. There were no power plants on

the Gambia's northern shore, in fact, no power plants anywhere except the small blot of yellow lights clustered
around Banjul. Only a few bare bulbs disturbed the darkness. I was sitting and talking to a man named Mamoudou
when the hotel's lights came on, and I heard a generator
whirring in the background.

"Oh you have the *ju-ju*," exclaimed Mamoudou, notic-
ing the charm on my ankle. "But you should not tell anyone
what it is for. You know they have the *ju-ju* for many things,
to protect against magic or for strength." He pointed at a
small leather pouch strapped to his muscular bicep. "If
someone knows what it is for they can defeat it." I agreed it
was an important secret to keep, and decided not to ask
what his *ju-ju* was for.

After dinner a kerosene lantern waited in front of my
room, and I got ready for bed by its flickering light, careful
not to set fire to the bed or the mosquito netting over it.
The room was stuffy, the windows had no screens, and the
door wouldn't lock. After trying to jam the bolt home for a
few minutes, working up a sweat in the process, I pulled the
door shut with a bungee cord and shrugged, figuring that
would just have to do.

Nervous about sleeping alone in the middle of Africa, I
closed the shutters, slathered myself in bug repellent and
went to bed. Immediately I began to pour sweat. It felt like
I was choking, smothering in the repellent. Soon the heat
was too much and I got up, flinging the shutters wide, but
even with the windows open, no breeze found its way into
the room. I lay on the foam mattress bathed in sweat,
thinking about hanging my mosquito net over a hammock
and taking my chances with the bugs and the open sky.
Then I sighed. Wasn't this what I'd longed for? That first
night upcountry, it felt like I was finally in Africa, and it was
miserably hot. But weariness crept over me, and after an
eternity I fell asleep, wishing for the morning to come.

I woke sometime in the middle of the night, filled with the violent urge to relieve myself. I thought for sure I'd already sweated out all the water I ever drank, but nature was intent on proving me wrong, and I found myself stumbling out to the hotel bathrooms at three in the morning. A sliver of moon shone overhead, illuminating the still scene in pale light. Dark trees and the shadows of broad leaves hung over the gray path, soundless in the moonbeams, and when I looked up, I saw there were a thousand stars.

• • •

"Does Zach chant at night?" asked one of the girls over breakfast.

I looked at her in confusion, and asked if she could repeat that bit.

"We heard him chanting last night, and it sounded like he was speaking in tongues." Zach had slept in one of the hotel *boukarous*, round huts common in West Africa, where the tops of the walls were open to let air and unholy curses flow freely.

"I've always thought he was the devil," I said and frowned at Zach, who grinned maniacally across the table. "But I've never heard him chanting." Maybe he'd been having a fit. Zach was mildly epileptic, and told me that he sometimes had seizures he didn't remember.

The roads worsened after we left Juffreh-Albreda, and away from the cool breezes of the Atlantic the sun revealed its full glory, baking the earth and our skins a deep red. The dry bush upcountry appeared dead, or perhaps it was only asleep and waiting for the rains.

Out here the presence of green things always pointed to a watering hole, or a small stream snaking through the dirt, or the Gambia River itself. Between these green islands, silence prevailed, and the hot breeze carried only the occasional birdsong or chirp of an insect. Thorn fences protected fields, cement was a rarity, and mud huts with thatched roofs clustered in the bush. We saw few people outside of village centers, and those who appeared passed slowly, perhaps stopping to gaze at us for a moment before moving on.

Our course left the river and traveled inland, on the path toward ancient stone circles, becoming dryer and more barren with every passing mile. The Gambian rainy season begins in May and early June, but the rains were still late and the land was parched, the air thick with anticipation as farmers waited for the lifeblood of the earth.

Late in the morning, our cars bumped into a group of featureless buildings clustered around the road, with a few cinder block affairs here and there to break the absolute monotony of dirt.

"This isn't the stone circles," we said, looking out at the dusty streets. "Is it?"

"No, this is Farafenni," said Bill. "You don't have to get out. I'm just making a call." He ducked into the darkened entrance of a GamTel call center, leaving the rest of us sitting in the van and sweating.

Across the street a man hawked cigarettes, matches, and lighters from a stand. Abby and Christina headed for their daily fix, both still unable to quit, finding it too easy to say, "I'll just buy one," and then smoke like a chimney. The moment they left the van, Farafenni's resident lunatic spotted the *tubabs* and approached eagerly, greeting us with shouts of welcome.

"Give me a cigarette," he cried, following the girls as they puffed away. "I was in America. I was in Spain. I was in Ireland. Give me a cigarette! I was in Spain. Give me a cigarette!" He smiled ingratiatingly and his black teeth showed as he hobbled after Christina on skinny legs.

"Why on earth were you in Spain?" demanded Christina, moving away even as she spoke.

"I was in Ireland! I was in Dublin!"

"Yes, but why?"

"I know Spanish. Give me a cigarette!" The rest of us watched the comedy unfolding, trying hard not to laugh as he danced in the middle of the street, prancing about with his arms and legs flapping. "I'm American," he cried. "Cigarette!"

We drove to Farafenni Secondary School for lunch, and when the meal ended I made the mistake of asking for directions to the bathroom. Shit stained the toilets in the men's room, and the sinks were dry. I looked at the toilets and thought better of it.

Farther along, the engine blew a gasket. A white jet of steam shot out from under the hood, and immediately the air conditioning sputtered to a halt. We sat on the roadside as the driver tried to repair it, but it was hopeless; we continued driving in the heat, the windows open to the furnace blast.

Two fuel pumps appeared even deeper in the bush, looking deserted until an attendant materialized from thin air. Gambians had the ability to magically appear when needed, though many also had the tendency to stick around when not. The ancient machines rattled to life as we sat and sweated, and I wondered where the fuel for these pumps came from. How often did a fuel truck drive this far out? There was nothing else in sight, just the two pumps and their attendant.

At the Wassu stone circles the sense of isolation was intense. The solid pillars of rust-red stood forlornly in a field of bare earth, guarded by a chicken wire fence, and collections of small, fist-sized rocks sat on top of each pillar, placed there for good luck. The pillars varied in height from those about knee-high to those that someone must have stood on tiptoe to place a rock on.

A small museum stood at the entrance to the site, its displays identical to those at Katchikally and the National

Museum. The curator appeared, and I wondered if he, like the gas station attendant, hung about in case tourists arrived. The road was empty in either direction as far as I could see. Did he sit there every day, just waiting on the occasional visitor? Maybe he lived in the scattering of mud houses in the distance, invisible except for metal roofs glinting in the sun.

The circles were burial grounds, with a central grave in each. Amy, the graduate student who was riding with us, said that only one grave had been excavated, leaving the rest undisturbed as part of a United Nations site. We nodded and took pictures, agreeing it was probably best to avoid provoking the ancestors by tossing the old bones about. We wandered from circle to circle, our voices and laughter almost profane in the silence. Here at last was something ancient, truly part of the past — and it was dead. Gambians no longer rested in circles like this, and the graves by the road into Banjul were the modern face of death in the Gambia. But the small stones on top… Those were newer, and I was sure that people still put them there for luck. I thought about leaving my own rock, to add to the protection of my *ju-ju*. I planned to swim again, and unless I took lessons, I'd need all the luck I could get.

A group of men began to dance by the entrance, inviting us to join them. Their dance resembled the quick steps of someone walking on hot sand, and only Casey joined in, hopping around like a mad kangaroo. The rest of us took pictures. We were *tubabs*. It was what we did best.

The land grew greener after we left Wassu, showing increasing signs of life, until finally water glinted through the trees. The van pulled up to a ferry crossing. The river had narrowed, and the ferry was only big enough for two cars at a time, leaving us at the mercy of small children as we watched it deposit a car on the opposite bank and make its slow way back across the river.

"Any pen? Any pen?" said the children.

Across the water the town of Janjanbureh, formerly Georgetown, also known as Jan-Jan Burreh, Janjanburray and Janjanbiray, sprawled along the shoreline of MacCarthy Island. I thought the town should have stuck to the old name — not out of any sense of imperialist superiority, but because nobody could decide how to spell the new one.

The town was the second largest in the Gambia, and housed the country's largest prison, but Bill had arranged other accommodations. Hard roads led to our hotel, a quiet place with small *boukarous* and neem trees spreading their broad branches above hammocks. The sign at the entrance read Baobalong Camp, and I wondered what a "baobalong" was as agama lizards ran about, peering at us from the walls and pumping their heads curiously. A single bulb hung from the ceiling in my room, and I was excited to see running water in the bathroom. All over the bathroom. The pipes below the sink emptied onto the floor, and the showerhead hung over the toilet. I scratched my head, puzzling over the logistics of taking a bath in this country, used the flush toilet (another wonder), and sat down to write in my journal.

I was still writing when I heard a sound approaching — first a gentle patter on the leaves all around, followed by the ping of impacts on the roof. Then I saw it: the first rain of the season. Outside the light turned yellow, and drops hung from the eaves, dripping like liquid gold. I could hear the others laughing in the shelter of the hotel's dining area, but I stood by myself, watching as the rains finally began and giving thanks for their cooling influence.

Arian and Steve, two volunteers from the Peace Corps, joined us at dinner. Peace Corps volunteers are not paid enough to pass up free food, and enjoy any chance to see fellow Americans. Between mouthfuls, they told us about their work as education volunteers, trying to teach young students about computers at a school that could only afford to power the machines for a few hours every week. It sounded harder than what we were doing, driving through a dusty land in relative comfort and staying in hotels with plenty of food. It didn't sound like something I could do, and didn't sound like something I wanted to try.

Termites crawled in the rotting rafters that night, dropping onto me as I tried to sleep. Slowly I drifted off to dreamland, and mosquitoes whined in the darkness above me, ignoring the fan that blew gently during the hotel's scant few hours of electricity. Later I would appreciate even simple amenities like this, and realize that things could be far worse in the bush. But I had no such appreciation that night. At the time I just thought it was inconvenient having termites on my face.

The fan turned off in the night, and I woke with the sudden warmth, aware that the land was still, the blackness outside deeper than anything I had ever seen. Even the mosquitoes had settled down for the night, and in the overwhelming silence I tossed and turned for a long time before I could find my way back to sleep.

• • •

We rose early, greeting the day and cramming breakfast down our throats. Some of the others had little appetite. Debbie had been sick during the drive upcountry, and Mary was ill the day before.

Outside the hotel the day was bright, the colors almost washed from the village as we followed men named Foday and Musa through Janjanbureh. A "freedom tree" stood in the center of town, where British soldiers once sat to keep watch for escaped slaves, and like the "freedom pole" in Albreda, any slave who made it to the tree would be declared free. The scraggly thing barely reached my chest, and Foday explained that the original tree died some years ago and was replaced by the current sapling.

When we'd paid sufficient respect to the new tree, our guides took us to Armitage High School, established in 1927, the school where Arian and Steve taught. Most of the students boarded at the school, their homes too isolated for them to walk in each day. Banjul was the only part of the country that swelled with people, Gambians who moved away from their homes to make a little money, trying to support those left behind. But everything upcountry seemed cut off by the bad roads and the bush, and the endless stillness lay like a veil between villages. I felt a small stab of pity, perhaps undeserved, for the inhabitants of a region so cut off from everything else.

Arian met us at the entrance, showing us the computer lab where she taught. Donated computers filled the room, a tiny generator provided power for a few hours every week, and as I looked at the dingy room I wondered how useful it could be for the average student at Armitage. Goats bounded about the campus, most of the classrooms were open to the air, and the computers seemed out of place. Could the students hope to use the skills they learned, or should the money be spent on a more practical project?

My steps fell unconsciously in the dust when we left the school, and Bill led us toward a cemetery on the edge of town. Foday and Musa were gone; Arian had left us at the school. We walked alone, strangers here, led by a man who lived in this country for two years when he was a Peace Corps volunteer. What had that been like for Bill, to try and make a home here?

The sun had bleached the land around the cemetery. Christian and Muslim graves mingled together, the graves untended, crumbling and broken by trees, and the tombstones showed signs of getting ready to fall apart and reveal the dead. It didn't take long to circle the cemetery, and when Bill asked if we wanted to see another school, no one but Debbie volunteered.

We were walking back when I heard the clang of a hammer. The sound grew louder near a shack by the side of the road, and when we stuck our heads inside, a short man straightened up from his work and put down a hammer to greet us. Corrugated metal made up the roof of the smith's shack. Its inside was black with soot and shadow where the tools of his trade hung from the rafters, and a fire burned in one corner, its flames licking at glowing coals, scorching the earth around it.

He spoke no English, so Bill translated as I asked questions. A member of the Mandinka tribe, Oumarou the blacksmith said he still made traditional tools like axes, and showed me the blade of the broken hoe he was busy repairing. I smiled and thanked him, waiting until Bill translated before leaving, wondering if I'd ever return. Did I want to come back this far, away from the coast, away from my friends and the comforts of home? Maybe there was more to be learned near Banjul, where the clash of the modern and the ancient was clearer. Or maybe that was my rationalizing a desire to stick close to air-conditioning. I wasn't sure.

Back at the Baobalong, Zach and I sat in our room, having strange conversations and singing all afternoon. When I went outside to sit in a hammock, the girls stared at me, asking what the hell we'd been doing in there.

"Singing," I said, putting on my headphones and leaning back in the hammock. I closed my eyes, Elvis began to play, and I started singing along.

"Andrew, are you chanting?" called one of the girls.

"Dammit," I yelled, not bothering to open my eyes. "You think everyone's chanting. I'm not Zach."

• • •

We left the hotel late in the afternoon and followed Bill to the waterfront, where a pirogue waited for us in the river. Like most watercraft in the Gambia, it was as much a work of art as a mode of transport: a carved man and woman guarded the top of the ladder down its side, and figures bearing jugs of water or playing instruments adorned the tree trunks that supported the cabin's roof. On the bow a carving of the Ninki-Nanka, a dragon that inhabits the river, stood guard with its toothy maw. The Ninki-Nanka likes to take children who become too confident and disobey their parents, venturing into the swamps around the river — the boogieman of the Gambia River.

Quietly the boat slid away from shore. The man at the stern guided it gently, one hand resting on the long oar he used to steer, and we stretched out on the roof with the relaxed air of people glad to be moving by something other than their own power. Monkeys hung in palm trees on the shore, dark lumps picking fleas from each other and watching our progress as a fisherman in a canoe went by and the boat cut a slim wake in the shimmering water. Below us the river alternated between olive and mocha, its colors shifting with the shadows on the water, winding lazily and taking its time westward to the sea.

"Hippos," someone said, and everyone grabbed their cameras as the boat slowed. There they were, just ahead of us, black blobs on the surface, bobbing a hundred feet away. They swam contentedly, but we knew better than to get too close to the most dangerous animal in Africa, content to watch from afar. Occasionally one of them raised its head and yawned, revealing long round teeth.

The boat turned back, snaking through the water until the boatman cut the engine and we drifted to a stop. I heard the sound of an anchor hitting the water. Three of the girls climbed on the railing, balancing while the rest of us shouted for them to jump, and then they leaped, sending up great splashes before they disappeared below the water's surface. After a moment they reappeared, swimming hard against the current, and climbed out one by one, dripping wet and grinning, leaving the railing free for me to climb up and jump, hanging in the air for an instant before I splashed down. Instantly the current swept me up, pulling me toward the back of the boat, and the river, which seemed so languid from above, showed its hidden strength. The brown water coursed over my limbs, and I stroked hard to stay in place.

We dove and swam, dove and swam, until everyone was tired and it was time to go back. The river had stolen Casey's *ju-ju* from her ankle, though we suspected the Ninki-Nanka was the true culprit. Just like the children the dragon liked to eat, we'd grown too confident, and this was a warning.

"It's a good thing you were wearing that *ju-ju*," I said. "Otherwise it would have taken you instead."

The boatmen pulled up the anchor and started the engine, taking us home as evening fell. The trees grew dark, suddenly shadow guardians of the riverbanks, their thin branches defined in perfect clarity as white egrets soared across the setting sun and disappeared, lost in the glimmer of the river and the yellow light in the sky. Slowly the sun sank, fading into the purple depths until only its aura remained to light our way into the dock.

We sat down to dinner and were just beginning to eat when a flying thing smacked into my arm, careened off, and fell on the table. Another hit my chest, and a third landed in my food. I picked it from the plate and saw a termite, waving its tiny legs at me. Suddenly dozens more flew in out of the dark, smacking into human obstacles or landing in our food and flopping around until they died. Responding to the ancient sign of the first rains, the termites had come out of their holes and now flew frantically for the hotel lights, colliding with anything in their path. They swarmed everywhere, in the air, in the food, on our clothes, in my hair...

"Oh God," I cried, "they're in my hair!"

It was impossible to stop them getting in the food, and I could feel them as I chewed, alive and squirming on my tongue. Finally I had to put my fork down, but when the meal ended and the termites settled down, we stayed up late playing games and laughing until I went to bed happy, content, not knowing what the next day would bring.

## CHAPTER TEN
# Return to Friendship

Huddled over the toilet the next morning and struggling to flush in time to puke my guts out, I began to regret my swim in the river. I'd bolted from bed the moment I woke, and now I could hear Zach laughing from the bedroom. In other circumstances I would have thought about punching him, but two things stopped me from doing it. I knew that if our roles were reversed I would be playing the jackass instead, and my stomach didn't let me want to do anything but empty it. The trip had finally caught up with me, and when I'd emptied the contents of my digestive tract into the sewers, I staggered out to where the others sat cheerfully eating breakfast.

"What's the matter, Andrew," said Bill, "are you not feeling well?"

"Urk," I said, and leaned against a tree to keep from collapsing.

"Here, have some of this." He tossed me a packet of oral rehydration salts. I tried some of the solution, but it tasted like seawater, and my stomach did a few somersaults in protest. Setting it aside, I decided I would wait until death before trying any more, and rode up front when we left Janjanbureh, taking the "sick seat" perpetually occupied by the sickest member of our group. In my lap I clutched a roll of toilet paper while my eyes scanned for the nearest foliage, just in case the need arose for an emergency pit stop.

I spent the rest of the morning in fear that I would have to make a mad dash for a roadside bush. We swerved from one side of the road to the other, my stomach lurched, and the car rocked as the wheels bounced through potholes. Sometimes a man on a bicycle passed by, the steady pumping of his legs propelling him faster than the car, and occasionally a broken-down van came in the opposite direction, appearing in the distance and slowly working its way over the road until it passed us and vanished in the dust. Then we continued in solitude, the only movement in the bush.

The horizon seemed to inch closer, reminding me of Bill's warning about the south bank road. The crest of every hill brought only the sight of another, more distant ridge, and I began to despair of ever reaching anywhere. Monkeys scampered in the bush, staring out at our passing, and their brown coats blended with the land, making them look like silent extensions of the trees. Farmers worked fields where the first shoots of bright green grass showed, steering wooden plows over earth that looked darker than before, washed by rains and turned up in long rows by the plows.

By the time we stopped for lunch it was miserably hot, and I groaned with more than sickness as I stumbled into a rustic compound of sunbaked brick. We sat Indian-style in the dirt of the front porch, legs crossed under flies that buzzed around us, and a Peace Corps volunteer came to welcome us to his village. He seemed to hardly notice the flies, or the children who gathered in the compound to stare, wide-eyed at the sight of so many *tubabs*. A matronly woman with broad shoulders and thick arms shifted in and out of the kitchen at the back of the house, carrying massive pots and occasionally stopping to shoo the children away. There was no breeze, and sweat trickled down my neck while the flies landed on my bare legs, staring up at me as if to say, "Are we driving you mad yet?"

"I'm just going to ignore them," I thought, waiting and waiting for lunch, feeling the small things crawl on my arms and legs. "I'm just going to ignore," and then I couldn't take it any longer and twitched wildly, flailing at the insects. They buzzed away, hovering out of reach before returning to torment me. Gambian flies were more brazen than their American cousins, knowing that most Gambians wouldn't bother to swat them.

The volunteer and Bill chatted endlessly to one side, going on and on about life as a volunteer in the village. I glared at them, blaming them for the wait, thinking that I would never want to live like this. How could they stand this, the interminable waiting, the bugs, and the children staring as you sweated in the heat? "Only an idiot would join the Peace Corps," I thought.

When lunch arrived, I ate two plates of vegetables and rice, shoveling it into my mouth in spite of the burning spices. Hours of waiting had cured my illness, replacing it with a hunger that would rule my days now and had made the others call me a bottomless pit the night before, when we tried to come up with nicknames as termites swarmed in the darkness.

Our route turned back toward the river after that, to land where flooded fields grew dark with rain. Long earth ridges broke their surfaces, and women walked along the ridges in single file, baskets balanced on their heads, their colorful skirts swaying above water that shimmered with reflections of the steel gray sky. I swooned when I saw my room at Tendaba Camp, perched on the river's edge. The lights came on at the flick of a switch, and stayed on. No termites fell from the ceiling, and the room was cool enough that I wouldn't die from dehydration while I slept. The shower didn't pour out over the toilet, and the sink didn't even empty out onto the floor. With the comfort of a new place, Zach and I spent the afternoon singing and shouting at each other in our room, and when I emerged the girls stared at me like I'd gone mad.

"Andrew," said Amanda, standing with her hands on her hips. "What on earth were you singing?"

"Country roads, take me home…"

"Uh-huh."

"To the place I belong…" Amanda rolled her eyes and went back inside. "West Virginia," I belted after her, "mountain mama, take me home, country roads…"

Night fell before dinner began, and with it came the bugs. Termites swarmed in the air above us, diving wildly and landing in our food, until I lost my appetite and went back to the room, where a mottled gecko squatted on the path and stared impudently up at me.

"Why aren't you doing your job?" I demanded. "Go eat some bugs, for God's sake."

• • •

The morning sun woke me, shining bright outside the quiet of my room. I felt rested for the first time since leaving the coast, my mood and body improved by a good night's sleep and a lack of insects disturbing my slumber. The sun rose higher, glaring outside our windows as we drove back into the interior, weaving south around the mangrove swamps. The road began to grow familiar, dimly remembered from our visit to Kanilai, but the land was greener than before, and farmers stood in their fields to watch our passing, pants rolled up above muddy feet.

It was hot again, and I dozed. Occasionally we stopped to refuel or use the nearest bush, and children appeared at every stop, staring and begging from window to window, their hands reaching into the van to grab at us.

"*Tubab, tubab,*" they cried.

"No, there is no pen," said Sarah.

"No dollar," said Holly. I just shut my window. The

children stared. A grasshopper dove in through an open window, clicking and buzzing madly. "Get it, get it!" cried the girls, and I reached back, grabbing the thing and tossing it out the window. The grasshopper flew off, over the heads of the children and into the bush. It was still hot, and I slept some more. The sky seemed a blaze of harsh light, endless above a land of washed-out color.

Early in the afternoon we arrived at Tumani Tenda, an ecotourism camp near a village of the same name. The name came from Tumani, a peanut-picker who once lived in the area, and the word *tenda*, which meant riverbank. A Koranic scholar named Alhadji Osman founded the village after he emigrated from Casamance, establishing it near a tributary of the Gambia River. The camp lay on the edge of a mangrove swamp, and I could smell saltwater on the wind. We were getting close to the coast.

The men at the camp took us to meet the *alkalo*, or village chief, who fanned himself on a porch surrounded by younger men listening to portable radios. Historically, newcomers asked the chief's permission to stay in village, and if the question is now largely ceremonial, out of politeness we asked anyway.

"*Alkalo*, thank you for welcoming us to your village," said Bill, who sat next to the *alkalo* while the rest of us squatted in the dirt. "How is your health? And your family?" Greetings were extremely important in the Gambia, done at much greater length than in America. All the formalities had to pass before getting down to business, so that we often sat for some time while Bill made the introductions and talked about the weather — especially when he greeted older men, the most respected members of Gambian society.

Bill spoke and one of the young men translated, the conversation flowing slower than molasses while we sat there and my butt went numb. I couldn't understand the *alkalo*'s words, but I knew what he was saying. The local languages all had their traditional greetings, and in Mandinka we had learned to ask about the health of everyone we met, to inquire if their family was all right, or if there was any trouble in their life, and to expect the reply that all was well. Bill was doing the same thing with the *alkalo*, who spoke the language of the Jola, the founders of the village.

"And these are the students," said Bill. The chief nodded, staring out at us with sharp eyes almost hidden in the wrinkles of his face. "They have each learned a bit of a local language," Bill continued, and I caught the words Wolof and Mandinka as he pointed to each of us, telling the chief which language we spoke. The *alkalo* went through the traditional greetings, switching to Mandinka when he came to me.

"*Salaam aaleekum*," I said, giving the Arabic for "Peace be upon you."

"*Maleekum salaam*," he replied, and asked if I were at peace.

"*Kayira dorong*," I said, meaning "peace only."

"*Suu moolu lee*? Where are the home people?"

"*I be jee*. They are there."

"*Kori tanante*?" said the *alkalo*, wondering if there was any evil in my life.

"*Tanante*," I said. "No evil."

"*Kayira tiiñanta*?"

"Uh... Bill?" I wasn't sure what that one meant.

"*Kayira dorong*," whispered Bill, who spoke a bit of all these languages.

"*Kayira dorong*," I mumbled. The chief smiled, nodding his head before he went on to the next student, and his smile widened when Bill presented a bag of bitter kola nuts. The caffeine-laden nut is chewed as a mild stimulant across West Africa, and was part of the original recipe for Coca-Cola, along with the coca leaf — hence the name Coca-

Cola. The chief took the nuts with great ceremony, clasping his hands and nodding his head, giving his blessing to our stay in his village.

Back at the lodge, one of the men poured *ataaya*, the sweet green tea used as a social drink in the Gambia and Senegal. He poured the thick liquid into a glass, then raised the glass and poured it into another, back and forth, back and forth to cool it, though the liquid was still steaming when he served, and scalded my tongue as I sipped.

After we finished the tea, the men talked about the importance of the swamp to their village as they readied two dugout canoes, pushing them into the water and waiting till we climbed aboard. With barely a sound, the canoes slipped away from the bank. This was only a small *bolong*, or tributary, but it smelled of the sea and snaked out of sight through the mangrove swamp. The murky water lay still all around us, colored dark by the rich mud, and the mangroves ran right down to the waterline, their thin, branch-like roots stretching into the shallows. To judge by the piles of shells on the camp's small beach, the oysters that grew on the mangrove roots were a staple of the village diet.

The men guided us quietly through the green corridors, their paddles dipping deep without as much as a splash. We were quiet as well, and once the camp faded from view, it seemed ethereal out there, with the rest of the country cut off behind a wall of green. We were lost in a world of our own, an endless maze, and nature demanded respect.

Finally, however, our reverence broke and we began to sing, loud and lustily, our voices warding off the river spirits, as if the preternatural silence of the place unnerved us. Sing-alongs are fun for the whole family, even a family with no known blood relation or musical ability, but it helps if those involved know the lyrics. After butchering tunes in tones that would make a choir director weep, we fell back on an old standby and began singing Disney songs. The girls performed flawlessly, while Zach and I whistled, hummed, belted out the chorus, and otherwise did our part to support the real stars. I'm convinced that all American females memorize the works of the Disney Corporation word for word, and it's possible that any man willing to duplicate this feat and endure odd looks from other men will find himself very popular with the ladies — or get odd looks from them as well. In either case, I'm not about to try. My singing sounds like a strangled rooster.

When our songs fell silent we took turns on lookout for the Ninki-Nanka. Somehow this felt like the perfect spot to taunt a supernatural being.

"The Ninki-Nanka," cried everyone in one canoe, pointing ahead.

"The Ninki-Nanka," echoed the other boat.

"Click," went our cameras.

Afternoon faded into evening back at the camp, and we played cards on rough mahogany benches, laughing in the cool air. Night fell and a few bulbs glowed, but between these islands of light the night grew dark as pitch. This still felt odd to my American sensibilities, so used to following illumination everywhere. Even paths shone with light in the States, but here we stumbled over roots and broken cement, cursing quietly.

When dinner arrived, tiny black spots crawled over the dining room floor. Closer inspections revealed shiny ants the size of carpet tacks, their bulbous heads tipped by giant pincers that seemed too large for their bodies. I felt a sting on my foot, and yelped in pain.

"Safari ants," said Bill, who liked stating the obvious. "Watch out, their bite is nasty." Another stung my toe, and the girls began to cry out. I felt more stings, but the ants were between food and me, and my stomach growled from the long day's journey. I hopped from one foot to the other as I tried to serve myself, and for a few seconds it worked, the ants unable to bite as the kitchen staff looked on like I'd gone mad. Then I felt more stings on my feet, the pain spreading up my legs, and had to retreat. Their bites felt like needles, but the pain subsided as we ate, keeping our feet off the floor and trying to enjoy another meal invaded by termites. Nothing kills the appetite like a dying insect in the stew.

To complete the insect menagerie, mosquitoes droned around us after dinner, their high-pitched whine piercing the night air. I still took my weekly malaria prophylaxis, but the doctor's warning came back to me. "This isn't one hundred percent," he'd said, and I thought about it on the walk to my room, scratching bites that itched something fierce and hoping I didn't feel the first hint of a fever. It was hard to tell in the constant heat, and maybe I was just being paranoid.

A single, bare, low-watt bulb hung from the ceiling in my room. It wasn't much, but it was better than nothing, and the bathrooms, open in the bush behind my room, were not so blessed. I clutched a flashlight and stumbled about wondering if emptying one's bowels in this country should present so many opportunities for injury.

Before I crawled under the mosquito net for the night, I took a shoe and paced the room, swatting insects and spiders as they scuttled for cover. I could hear Zach doing the same next door, and the occasional "thwack" of his shoe announced the death of another critter.

"Come see this bug's guts," shouted Zach, his voice triumphant. Rolling my eyes, I went next door and found him crouched over a black cockroach, its pink organs spreading out of its broken shell. Bugs should never be large enough to identify their intestines. I shuddered, went back to my room and redoubled my efforts.

At last all the visible insects were splattered against the walls, and I climbed into bed. There were no rafters for termites to fall from, the rains had cooled the air to just below the boiling point, and with the weariness of a long day on the road I slept soundly in the quiet of the bush.

• • •

Morning found us rising early to follow a man named Oumarou into the forest, rustling the thick carpet of leaves on the dry ground.

"We use the forest," said Oumarou, "but we also must keep it alive." The Gambia suffers steady deforestation as people cut wood for fuel and houses, and the villagers had been stressing their relationship with the forest since we arrived. If Abuko was what a Gambia without humanity would look like, the forest here was a much more likely compromise — a Gambia that wasn't being washed into the sea because ground cover no longer existed, but that still provided succor for the people living there. But how much was it tailored to the tourists they hoped to attract? I knew visitors could pay to take part in "traditional" village activities, and the things we did probably came with the price of our stay. Part of me wondered how much of this was real, and part of me wished I wasn't so cynical.

Another part of me decided to enjoy the wandering tour, and a fourth part — my stomach — reminded me it was almost time to eat. These last two voices, the pragmatic and the hungry, were the ones I listened to the most.

While I mused, Oumarou stopped to pick some dark seedpods off the ground and peel the thick skin open, holding the pods out to us and revealing a bright yellow powder around the seeds.

"You can just eat it," he said. Casey made a face, and nobody else looked eager to try, but I took a wad of the yellow stuff and ran it between my fingers. It felt like thick, clumped flour, and tasted like a cake, sweet and delectable on my tongue.

"You guys sure you don't want to try this?" I said, taking more. "It's very good."

"No, Andrew," said Abby, "but you go right ahead."

"I will," I said, finishing the rest and looking around for more.

We left the forest for the fields, moving single-file along ridges in soon-to-be-flooded rice paddies. In the hot sun of the open fields, saplings stood in long rows of ridged earth, looking faint and weary above the hard ground. The rains had started, that much was true, but only barely. I didn't envy the women who bent and struck at the dirt with short-handled hoes, moving rhythmically across their fields.

In the village itself, chickens scratched and pecked, running about as our guide showed us a communal chicken coop among the eroding mud walls of thatched huts. It seemed ancient. African villages all look like they've been there forever, having sprung from the earth and decided to stick around until they collapse back into it. The impression becomes ridiculous when you realize that villages made entirely of mud bricks will fall apart and be replaced after three or four rainy seasons. Tumani Tenda was certainly one of those villages. Alhadji Osman had founded the village only thirty years before, but in spite of that it projected an aura of great age.

Oumarou waved goodbye after the tour, and we piled into the van. It was time to head home, and home meant the Friendship Hotel. Strange to call a place we'd only been for two weeks "home," but that was the word on our lips as we bounced toward the coast. Only thirty miles lay between Tumani Tenda and Bakau, on relatively good roads, and the trip passed quickly. When we joined the main route I saw potholes I recognized and sighed in relief, looking forward to a familiar place to rest my head. After the rough roads and sickness of the past week, it was good to be back in room 313 and see Kawsu smiling down below, even as I ducked into the room when Ami called out for pens. Air conditioning never felt so wonderful, and suddenly the Friendship seemed like the epitome of decadence. We had good food and not one termite for dinner, decent bathrooms (though the shower had backed up and the toilet seat kept falling off), and safe drinking water, at least safe enough for me. I'd been in the Gambia for three weeks, but it seemed longer, like we'd adjusted a bit to life in a strange land, or like the land itself wasn't all that strange.

And the beach greeted us the next day, the white surf charging up the smooth sand as I ordered my usual meal of greasy chicken, eating greedily and watching horses trot past, feeling the sea breeze against my skin. I knew I would have to work tomorrow, beginning my research with artisans. I hoped to find an answer to the question of how they survived in a modern world, but for the moment I relaxed at Leybato, tired and sore from the road, simply enjoying the sun and the sand. The masseuses had returned, offering massages to the girls who lay on the beach, letting the bumps of the road fade away, and when I finished my chicken the woman at the bar slid another piece onto my plate, smiling as I thanked her. My reputation had preceded me.

"Things are looking up," I thought, digging into the second helping, putting tomorrow off as long as possible.

## CHAPTER ELEVEN
# Silver and Gold

Monday found me unsure, left to my own devices as the final leg of our tour began. For the remaining four weeks we would pursue our own projects, set our own schedules, and wander about like lost sheep. I would even have the room to myself, and wouldn't have anyone to help keep an eye out for Ami, because Zach and Christina planned to spend the time upcountry, studying archeology at Juffreh instead of anthropology with the rest of us.

On Tuesday Bakary Sidibeh would take Amanda and me to Tanje, to meet with craftsmen for my work, and visit traditional healers for hers. But on Monday we sat at the hotel, wondering what we were supposed to be doing. I felt guilty just sitting there, like I should be working on *something*. I just couldn't figure out *what*.

By noon Bill had had enough, and told us to go to Timbooktoo. "Why don't you go to Timbooktoo," he said, meaning, "Get your asses out and do something."

Timbooktoo wasn't the legendary city of ancient fame, but a small bookstore on the road to Leybato. We had to skirt piles of rubble along the way, careful to dodge the cars that whizzed past, intent on vehicular mayhem, and when we got there the store was the charming type that you expect to find tucked away in America, hidden in some gentrified hamlet or college town where local eccentricities still outshine big business. It had a large section devoted to Gambian authors, and more books on Africa than one normally finds in larger stores. Out front, stacks of local newspapers sported pictures of Yahya Jammeh, though it occurred to me they might do so more because of Jammeh's habit of imprisoning opposition journalists than out of any real love for the man. In either case, there wasn't much to be found on Gambian crafts, and before long I retreated to the comfort of the hotel, waiting anxiously for tomorrow.

• • •

Bakary turned off the road near Tanje, driving into a small cluster of low mud buildings. We had driven south from Bakau that morning, riding in Bakary's old Mercedes, which was of the large type favored by dictators the world over.

"A traditional healer lives here," said Bakary as he cut the engine and led us into the compound. Amanda wanted to work with traditional healers, so I sat down while she and Bakary went inside to talk with him.

Withered old grannies, mothers with sick children, cripples, and men with hacking coughs crowded the dirty yard. A tapestry hung outside the door, crudely depicting the ailments the healer could cure, and I stared at it, marveling at the simplicity of a catalog that illiterate customers could point to when they needed to identify symptoms. It showed men bent over and vomiting, men taking obviously uncomfortable shits on pit latrines, women fainting, and babies starving. In one picture, a disembodied hand attacked a man with a knife. In another, a neighbor cast a spell on an unsuspecting woman. Surrounded by the sick and dying, I wondered if Amanda would learn witchcraft.

Flies buzzed in the air, the black spots landing on Gambians who made no attempt to shake them off. Except for the insects and the wail of an unhappy baby, the compound was quiet. I twitched, swatting flies and dozing in the heat until Amanda emerged and we left, driving south to the Tanje Village Museum.

Ousman Jadama, the assistant to museum founder Abdoulie Bayo, greeted us at the entrance and led us inside. When he built the museum, Bayo wanted to show the elements of a traditional African village, from its *boukarous* to the craftsmen I'd come to see. I imagined it could represent a village, if the typical village were built out of concrete and completely deserted, bereft of its goats and children playing in the street. The displays looked the same as the other museums I'd seen, in a depressingly small-town kind of way, though there was no *kangkurao* to be seen.

One of the blacksmiths huddled over his forge at the back of the museum: a short, muscular man named Aggi Kanteh, whose poor English made for a brief conversation. But it was enough to learn that he and his brother Modou — who was absent — made mostly jewelry, and far less weaponry than I'd hoped.

"Some work more in blacksmithing, some in gold and silver," said Aggi. His small forge sat under a thatched roof, the furnace made of hardened earth black with soot, and tools hung from the ceiling. A hollowed-out log served as a trough for cooling red-hot iron, and a pair of leather bellows rested by an anvil. "We wet the bellows to soften them," said Aggi, splashing water to demonstrate.

When I rose and thanked him, he said I should come back and talk to his brother Modou, who knew more about blacksmithing. Modou had been taught by their father, also Modou Kanteh, who trained the older brother and died before he could teach Aggi.

The museum's resident weaver sat cross-legged at his loom nearby, working the shuttle back and forth, adding strand after strand of cotton thread. His English was better than Aggi's, and after he introduced himself as Ousman we chatted in the shade, examining the goods he had laid out.

While we talked his apprentice, a young man in his late teens, sat down and took over at the loom. Only men weave in the Gambia — the women help prepare the materials — and Ousman came from a clan of weavers, having learned from the elders as soon as he was old enough. They taught him how to behave, how to be patient and calm, and when they were satisfied with his work, they called all the elders together for a graduation.

"And then you are a weaver," said Ousman, snapping his fingers and spreading his hands. I smiled and rose, stretching stiff limbs, thanking Ousman and telling him I would be back. I wanted to stay longer, but Amanda and Bakary waited by the car.

"You want to see the rooms?" said Bakary. I was still weighing Bill's idea about staying upcountry or at Tanje, and I peered into the darkened *boukarous*, noting the lack of electricity and the bathrooms in the woods out back.

It wasn't the rustic nature so much as the isolation that turned me off. I knew that if I left the busy hubs, it would be hard to travel anywhere else. Transportation wasn't easy, and there was work to be done. Besides, I told myself, the life of coastal artisans intrigued me, making me wonder how they managed in a world that changed every day, affecting a way of life that existed for generations.

"I don't think I'll stay here," I said to Bakary, and we left Tanje, driving south along the road toward Gunjur, where sea-green flags flew by the side of the road, flapping in the wind atop mosques and schools.

"You see those flags?" said Bakary. "That's the color of the president's party. They mean the people here support him."

All along the route, schoolchildren stood by the roadside, their matching uniforms bright in the sun. "They are waiting for the president's procession," said Bakary. "They have been waiting all day, most likely." Seemed unfair to me. It was too hot to stand in the sun all day, unable to take a breather because you had to wait on some pompous official in his Mercedes.

"There are elections coming up," Bakary said when we caught sight of the procession. "He will be arriving to speak soon. Do you want to go see him?"

Amanda and I looked at each other and shrugged.

"It's okay," said Amanda.

"We've been to his parties," I added. "We don't need to see him again."

After that we headed inland, trading the sea breeze for landscapes where shoots of new growth barely eased the harshness. Slowly the land was coming alive, still hesitant to show its softer side, and rows of mud bricks lay drying in the sun, near shallow pits that farmers dug to harvest the mud. The bricks would go toward new houses soon, to be washed away in the rains.

The town of Brikama waited in the sun, sprawling around us ten miles inland. We'd seen bits of it when we drove to Kanilai, but now the town seemed to go on forever, big, brawling, alive with noise and heat in a swirl of dust. It had a kind of raw beauty that in another place might be ugly.

Crowds waited outside another healer's house, and Amanda looked in dismay at the huddled masses, the eager and the desperate spread all over the yard. Bakary poked his head in to see if the man could spare a moment, but there was no luck, and we left.

"Do you want to talk to the men who work with iron?" said Bakary, and he pointed at a group of young men working around half-finished doors in the dust. Bright blue sparks flashed where they put their arc welders to the metal, cutting and attaching geometric patterns.

"No," I shook my head, "just the traditional crafts." It was the romance of it that appealed to me. Men pounding at a forge, or making cloth on a loom like the one their grandfather used — that was foreign and strange to me. There was something much less exotic about using an electrical arc welder to make a door, no matter how elegant the end product might be.

• • •

I left the hotel early the next morning, walking slowly to the NCAC's office on Kairaba Avenue. Almost nothing moved in the morning calm, but a few young men lounged under a baobab, watching me and calling, "*Tubab, tubab!*" The Gambians in the neighborhood were a friendly lot, but a conversation might start with inquiries about my health, and end with them asking for money.

"Hello, *tubab*, how is the day?" called the men.

"Oh fine, thank you. How are you today?"

"Fine. Give me dollar!"

"Why?"

They stared blankly, and then shouted again.

"Give me dollar!" Not even a "please." I wanted to tell them their flawless logic had overwhelmed my objections, and they should help themselves to my money, but I refrained.

"Sorry, there is no dollar," I said, and hurried on.

That morning Bill had suggested, in that subtle way of his, that I spend some time going over the NCAC library to try and find something on traditional crafts in the Gambia. What I found, when I reached their office on Kairaba, was that work would go nowhere if I stuck to books. Musty old tomes filled the library, reminding me of books that belonged to my paternal grandparents. They came from Maine, and in true Maine tradition never threw anything away. When my grandfather died, the barn he owned was full of old odds and ends: an organ, rusting farm tools, empty barrels, a pickup truck that didn't run, children's games, and enough furniture to fill a house. In a set of shelves we found schoolbooks from decades before, covered and forgotten in the dark. The books in the library had the same smell, the smell of something unused, left there and forgotten, as much a part of the dusty past as the history they contained.

The women cleaning the compound smiled at me and bustled in and out, scrubbing the floors and sweeping the dirt outside. I was supposed to meet with office director Balla Saho and his assistant Yamin Yarbo, but they were nowhere in sight. The electricity had gone out, and I sat by the open door, reading and sweating in heat that could easily have been worse. The *harmattan* still blew some days, so that a haze seemed to blanket the sky, and the faint figures of mango leaves danced on the pages.

"Okay, we can go?" said Balla, appearing suddenly with Yamin. "You want to go to the silversmiths, yes?"

"Yes," I said, eager to begin. I hadn't seen the silversmiths since the first time we drove over the bridge, and I hoped they would remember me.

When Balla, Yamin, and I arrived, the silversmiths sat in their cage, the clang of their hammers sharp in the air. Balla had things to do in the museum — the work of a government bureaucrat is never done — so Yamin and I poked our heads through the enclosure door, and saw the old man in the same position I'd seen him in weeks before, seeming not to have moved since then. He looked up at the sound of visitors and reached out to shake my hand, introducing himself as Mbaie Mbowe, his hand thick and scarred in mine.

"And how do you spell that?" I asked, not at all sure I would get his name right. My ongoing quest to grasp unfamiliar Gambian names was complicated by the fact that they rarely agreed on how to spell them. They'd relied on oral history for centuries — half the population is still illiterate — and when names are rarely written, spelling is less important than pronunciation.

"M, b…" He paused to think about it. "A, i, e," he continued, while I scribbled in my notebook.

"Mbaie," I repeated, underlining it for emphasis.

"Or Baie," he added, just to confuse me. Then he introduced me to Jaja Touray, the middle-aged man sitting next to him, and Samba Chaum, the young man bent over an anvil in the corner.

"*Salaam aaleekum*," I said, and the men muttered "*Maleekum salaam*."

"Okay, I will wait," said Yamin, retreating as Samba pulled up a chair. I sat down, but neither the silversmiths nor I seemed to know what came next.

A small pile of charcoal burned in a hole in the floor, glowing orange in its depths, and a pipe ran out of the hearth, up to a hand-cranked fan that Samba began to turn, blowing fresh oxygen to the center of the coals. The fire burned red-hot, brighter and brighter until Samba took a silver ingot, about the size of my little finger, and placed it on the coals. He turned the crank again, and the metal glowed with the heat of the flame. With a pair of tongs Samba pulled the ingot out and plunged it into a bucket of water. The metal hissed for a moment before he laid it on an anvil and began to pound, his hammer striking blow after blow, the sound ringing in the air. Slowly the metal gave way under the hammer as Samba shaped it, repeating the process when the metal grew unwieldy, until finally it turned into a bangle.

Sitting in a corner, scribbling notes and taking pictures, I learned that the men were members of the Gambian Gold and Silversmiths Association (GGSSA), an organization founded to pass on the trade and obtain materials and tools for the smiths. Baie had been the president for the last three years, but he spent most of his time at the shop because it was a good place to teach.

"You know, the group was started by our fathers," said Baie. "They founded it as a cooperative in the early forties, to give access to government loans. But then it was dormant for many years, when I was in Senegal. We began to revive it when I returned from Senegal."

"Is it very big?"

"Hmm? Yes, it is very big, hundreds of members in Banjul and nearby. And we have a bank account!" He added this last bit with pride, puffing out his chest and smiling. "We are writing a proposal for a training center. If the government gives us money, we will build it in Brikama."

While I sat in the tiny workshop, almost blocking the door, Yamin waited outside. I felt bad keeping him for so long, but he said it was okay, grinning when I ran out of questions and emerged from the cage.

"You are ready? You want to see the market?" He meant Albert Market, which nestled up against the Atlantic, where the surf curved away from the ocean and into the mouth of the Gambia River. The market was a mass of shops, some concrete and metal, but most made of scrap wood and torn canvas; in the most thickly packed areas, the canvas stretched across the narrow walkways, forming dark corridors to swallow us up.

The vendors ignored me in the regular market, but as soon as I entered the craft market the *tubab* alert went out and the owner of every shop shouted, beckoning me to come and look, come and see. I peered into shops filled with clothes too bright to imagine, senses overwhelmed by colors, by whirling paintings and twisted carvings, and by a hundred voices clamoring for attention. I pushed on, unable to stop, my mind trying to make sense of the overload. Finally, down a tiny alley at the very back of the market, I paused to look at a cloth map of Africa. Each country was a different brightly patterned fabric, woven together into the shape of the continent — a reminder that despite the outsider's view of Africa, it wasn't all the same.

Seeing me looking at the map, the fat woman in the stall grabbed my arm, smiling broadly and pulling me in.

"My brother," she cried. "You like? I give you good price!"

"Good price? You give me good price? How much is good price?" Being in the Gambia had seriously affected my grammar.

"Two hundred for you, my brother!"

"Two hundred? No, two hundred is too much." I offered one hundred, and her face fell.

"My brother, that is too little. That is not good price. One hundred eighty."

"No, one twenty," I countered, playing the game.

"One hundred fifty."

"No, one twenty." I was arguing over a dollar here, but the Gambia had also altered my sense of the hard bargain.

"Oh, that is still too little," she complained. "For one twenty, I do not eat. Here, I give you free necklace if you buy. One hundred fifty and free necklace!" This was too much to resist. I handed over the money and stuffed the map into my bag.

"We had better go now," I muttered to Yamin, waiting patiently outside. "Or I may never leave."

• • •

As the other students and I spent our time outside and adapted to the climate, our air-conditioned rooms grew increasingly frigid. I slept most nights curled under blankets that had spent the first two weeks of my stay shoved to the foot of the bed, but now sheltered me from the cold air. This was still no reason to turn the air conditioning off. You should never look a gift horse in the mouth, and the power still went out occasionally, though we no longer complained, we just rolled over and threw off the sheets when it did.

The day after I visited the silversmiths I read the papers Bakary had given me on crafts. I told myself it was work, but I spent my time by the pool, reading a little, talking with the others, eating whenever I wasn't talking, and trying not to fall asleep before remembering to apply sunscreen. A lazy day, but even Bill agreed I'd been busy so far. "One day off won't hurt," I reasoned, but still felt a twinge of guilt as I went to bed. My parents, I think, had done a good job instilling a Puritan work ethic in me.

I woke determined to get out and do something, even if it was so bright the sun blinded me when the door swung open. Abby, Amanda, and I left early for the NCAC, taking a dirt track behind the Friendship. The girls said this was a shorter route, and I have a bad habit, softened over the years but still there, of quietly assuming that other people know what they're doing. It's never gotten me into serious trouble, but it's one of those things that could easily go bad in the wrong circumstances — a dark alley, a hiking trip in the woods, or anything that relies on judgment to keep things from going awry. If other people don't know what they're doing, I'll happily follow along, even as I complain that we've seen that tree before, or wonder if a mountain lion is going to eat us.

"This is not shorter," I muttered, trudging behind the girls and feeling the sun on my back. The sky blazed even though it was only mid-morning, and I had the distinct impression that we would die if we didn't get to shade soon — not an impression you should have if you're only walking a mile and a half.

When Yamin and Balla arrived at the office, I waved goodbye to the girls and climbed into Yamin's car, which sputtered out of the compound. We headed south to meet a woodcarver named Saikouba Ceesay in Senegambia, an area near the hotel that hosted the ambassador's party.

When I followed Yamin out of the heat and into the

woodcarver's darkened shop, Saikouba sat in Senegambia's craft market, surrounded by his work. Lions, tigers, and elephants stared at us; masks frowned down from the walls, or twisted their faces in wild grimaces, lips pursed and brows furrowed. I hoped one of the tigers would come to life, leap from the shelf and attack. After all, what was a trip to Africa without an animal attack?

Saikouba welcomed me and began to talk about his life, which hadn't started in his current trade. Most crafts in the Gambia passed from father to son, and I'd assumed his father would have been a carver. But the man was a Mandinka farmer, making enough to support the family, but poor enough that Saikouba had no formal schooling.

"There is no money in farming," he said sadly. "It is very difficult for thirty years because of drought."

He'd worked for years as a tailor, then as a vendor in Brikama, before he fell in love with the carvings he sold, the wood polished to a bright sheen and almost alive in the small shop. He showed me the chisels and the *deno*, a small ax with a curved blade, that he used to carve his work, and the shoe polish that he used to color the wood. Carvers used to make their own paint, but there was little need for that in the age of mass-produced alternatives.

"This is rosewood," he said, picking up a piece and cradling it in his hands. "But we call it mahogany for the tourists." There was the charcoal tree, which the carvers called teak, and the bush mango. "That is very good for drums," said Ceesay, "and also statues." Ebony, which couldn't be found in the area, came from Senegal and Mali.

"I always had it in my mind that one day I must do this thing," said Saikouba when I asked how he began to carve. One day the inspiration just came, and he began carving a tiny mask for a necklace. A bumster — a tout, a beach bum — bought it, sold it, and brought back ten dalasi for Saikouba. The next day he made five pieces, and the day after that, ten. They sold well, better than his other goods, and he began to make bigger figures and masks. It might take him two weeks to make an exhibition piece, but a piece or two a day turned out all right for tourists.

"And a very good doll maker, who had a stall across from me, encouraged me," said Ceesay, smiling at the memory. He had worked for a while beside the silversmiths at the National Museum, but it was not a good place for business. Tourists wanted to buy carvings, not go to museums.

While at the museum, Ceesay began to train a boy named Sidie, who was very serious about learning to carve wood. The "boy" was now thirty or thirty-five — Saikouba didn't know for sure — and nowhere in evidence, spending more time doing carpentry than working in the shop.

"You can only learn the basics from a teacher," said Saikouba. "He can only teach you so much."

By the time I met him, Saikouba was famous enough that the Taiwanese ambassador wanted him to make replicas of traditional Taiwanese art. He'd helped found a society for Gambian sculptors, and his concerns were those of continuing his craft: fighting middlemen who pretended to make the goods they sold, displaying his work at exhibitions, looking at the international market, and training young people to take on the trade.

To hear him talk, it was all very businesslike and mundane, and even as I looked at the dark wood I wondered where I could find the exotic Gambia I'd so eagerly pictured. It felt as if there was a veil over my eyes, and I kept expecting it to be pulled back, revealing the Africa I'd waited for. But I'd made a mistake all along, refusing to see the country for what it really was, wanting only to see the Africa of films and Ernest Hemingway novels. Truth, as always, was more complicated, and like anything that's complicated, it took longer to see.

• • •

It was just after prayer time when Yamin and I drove into Banjul, and the street was full of men in white robes, returning from the mosque. Baie, Samba, and Jaja smiled to see me, taking their seats in the workshop and asking how I was. Proudly Baie showed me faded pictures on the wall, images of him and Jaja standing with the president. Baie was only two years older than my father, but he looked much older, his face more heavily lined, his hair grayer, the result of a lifetime spent over an anvil. He began to learn silversmithing at eight, apprenticed to his uncle Serna Samba, who lived in the same compound as Baie's father.

"My father was a mechanic," explained Baie. "So my uncle taught me." Training started with copper, and it took him six years before Serna trusted him with silver. "You have to be obedient," said Baie, pursing his lips. "You must obey everything! You must clean the shop, and you must do chores. Anything the master says, you must do." He frowned. "But you must be honest and sincere in yourself. Materials are expensive! Apprentices sometimes steal, and then they must be punished." I nodded in what I thought was an understanding manner.

"I left school in 1964 and tried to get a job," said Baie, pursing his lips again and peering into the distant memory. "But there was no luck, so I went back to work as a partner with my uncle. Then in 1965 I went to Senegal to get my qualifications to become a smith. Many Mauritanian silversmiths came to the Gambia — and Senegalese, and Guineans. It was hard to start a business when I returned from Senegal, and it is very difficult to import silver, because the rate on the dalasi is not good."

I asked if the difficulties were affecting the passing of secrets from father to son.

"Some people are choosing to go to school and other jobs," Baie said thoughtfully. "And not everyone marries a woman in a silversmith family. It is changing. That is one reason why we want to build the training center."

I spent hours crouched in the tiny shop, watching the men work and jotting down notes as the sun fell from the sky, the shadows shifting across the yard. Finally it was time to leave, and Samba helped me catch a taxi to Bakau — which cost five dalasi — in the taxi park where cars coughed blue smoke across the street. We went from van to van until we found one heading in the right direction, and there was just enough space for me to crouch in the back, squeezed between the other passengers as the car pulled out. In the dust, I watched Samba wave goodbye and disappear from view.

Zach had just gotten back when I walked into the room. He spent his time upcountry now, digging in the hot sun with Christina, and every weekend they retreated to the coast, desperately relaxing in Bakau's air conditioning.

"How was Juffreh?" I asked, throwing down my pack and letting loose a sigh of relief.

"It was hot," said Zach. "Very hot." He looked a little peaked, like he wasn't too sure he made the right choice heading upcountry. I smiled at him, as if to say it was his own damn fault, because what kind of lunatic sits out in the sun all day? And then I remembered that was exactly what I'd planned for tomorrow.

## CHAPTER TWELVE
# My Father before Me

Ahead of me, Casey's flip-flops kicked up sand, making smacking sounds when they hit her feet. We followed Bill through the streets near the hotel, going to meet Gibril, an old friend whose young son was one of the many Boubacars we knew around Bakau. Casey wanted to talk to Gibril's wives about polygamy, and I needed to pick up Boubacar for translation. I was going to talk to a leatherworker, and heard he didn't speak much English.

I felt better about work now that I had several contacts under my belt. The nervousness and nagging guilt were fading, replaced by confidence. Even if I couldn't quite put my finger on it, I sensed the long days of sunshine and friendly smiles changing me. But today was overcast, and we walked through the quiet streets under skies clouded with gray. The air was cool. Gibril lived on a street behind the hotel, where his family occupied several small buildings around the usual common area, and he greeted us when we entered.

"Come, come," said Gibril, who wore a robe over his belly and pulled me into one of the buildings, throwing back the curtain across its entrance as Bill and Casey went off to talk to his wives. A large bowl of pasty gray mush sat on a table.

"That is the *fufu*," said Gibril, watching me. "You should have breakfast!"

I had heard of *fufu*, a common dish across West Africa, though there seemed to be some debate over the exact nature of the dish. It was sometimes described as porridge, and other times as a thick paste of boiled root vegetables; the only thing anyone could agree on was that it formed a staple of the local diet.

Tentatively, I picked up a spoon and took a mouthful. It tasted like mush in a bowl, slightly sweet and thick as I chewed unexpected lumps of flour. This was definitely the porridge type of *fufu*.

"Mmm, s'good," I mumbled, swallowing and doing my best to grin. I took another spoonful as Gibril watched, but then he left the room to see how Casey was getting on with the women. I took a few more bites out of politeness, and put the spoon down. It was enough to make me miss Tang for breakfast, and I got up with perhaps a bit too much eagerness when Boubacar arrived, following him out and waving goodbye to Gibril.

The leatherworker sat in a corrugated metal hut nearby, squatting cross-legged on a mat. An old man, or aged prematurely by the harshness of his life, he held a dowel in his hands, sawing around one end with a small hacksaw. He nodded at us and stopped for a moment to shake my hand, introducing himself as Lamin Fatty.

"What is he making?" I asked Boubacar, pointing at the wood.

"It is a spear," said Boubacar, "for the tourists."

When Fatty had sawed all the way around the dowel, he took a knife and hammer, tapping the blade against the end to shear the wood from the outer edge. He kept turning the spear shaft, cutting bits of wood off until it sported a circular nub at one end. When he finished he laid it aside and reached for another rod, putting it between his toes and sawing vigorously. Then the saw went down again, replaced by the hammer and sharp knife, Fatty cutting bits until he reached for the next dowel.

"I will give them to a man who sells them to tourists," said Fatty as Boubacar translated. "Tourists like to buy things that are African. I used to make spears for the villagers, now I make these." He patted the pile beside him.

I was almost disappointed to see him making things for tourists, even if I had to admit I was one, and I asked what else he made.

"Knife handles, sheathes. Sometimes a Fula orders a saddle for a horse." He meant a member of the Fulani tribe, a pastoral group spread across West Africa. But the last Fula who ordered a saddle gave him nothing up front, and leather was expensive. "The best leather must be imported from Senegal," said Fatty, reaching for another dowel.

His family broke the mold of one family, one craft, and had carved wood and worked leather as far back as he knew. His father made shoes and *ju-jus*, not things for tourists. The old man was dead now, and shortly after his death Fatty came to live in Bakau with his mother and family, working every day in the small shack. Now he had two teenage sons, Muhamed and Brahima, and I asked if he taught the boys his craft.

"I will teach them," said Lamin, "but I want Muhamed to find a better job, because I never went to school." A third son was still a baby. "I will teach him, too, if he wants to learn," said Fatty, but his daughters Fanta, Mansata, Uday, and Binta wouldn't learn the trade. This was men's work.

As I sat listening, a young man came with the contents of a *ju-ju*, the pale paper covered in Arabic figures that contained a charm. He asked Fatty to make a cover, which Fatty said would cost five dalasi, and the leatherworker set down his tools, wrapped the paper in a cloth rubbed with honey, covered it in hide, and sewed it up with a bright nylon string, melting the string to seal it. Finally, he poked two holes in the cover, cut a thin hide strip, and passed it through the holes, tying it into a loop and handing it to the young man, who paid up and left.

Reaching into his shack, Fatty rummaged around for a moment and pulled out a sword in a black leather sheath. The blade was rough and dark with rust, hammered out into a thin curve of uneven metal — a ceremonial thing, not sharpened well and never meant for battle.

"How much for a sheath?" I asked, leaning forward eagerly. Mighty had bought me a cutlass — everyone in the Gambia called machetes cutlasses — and I wanted to give it the finest case around.

Fatty pondered for a moment, stroked his chin and told me it would cost twenty dollars. "Too much," I thought. The machete cost a quarter of that.

Another young man arrived, carrying a metal charm to go inside a *ju-ju*, and he looked oddly at me, as if wondering why this strange *tubab* was squatting with a notebook in front of the leather man's stall. Again I wasn't allowed to know what danger the charm protected against, because then I could use the knowledge against him.

When Fatty finished and the man left, a woman asked him to make a covering for yet another *ju-ju*, holding up a string with five charms already on it. The old *ju-jus* were dark, their leather almost black with age.

"Is there a market for African things in America?" said Fatty, peering at me hopefully.

"He says he wants to make money and work in a richer country," said Boubacar. I shook my head, not sure what to tell him. Maybe Westerners would pay for his goods, but the difficulty of getting them there…

When the interview ended, I shook Fatty's hand and rose, giving him something for his time.

"Boubacar, thank you very much for your help," I said, and pulled out a twenty-five dalasi note. He nodded gravely and turned back toward home, leaving me by the Friendship's gate. The hotel was almost deserted, the rooms quiet, the other students at the beach. I found Isaac with a pair of kittens crawling all over him, the offspring of stray cats that prowled the hotel yard.

"You're going to get ringworm," I said. "You don't know where those things have been."

Isaac grinned toothily. "But they're so cute," he said, holding one up. "Look at 'em!"

I had to admit they were cute, even if one of them looked like it had mange. Telling him not to complain to me when he caught something, I left Isaac to his fleabags and went to change. I was just at my door when I heard a bellow down below.

"Demba! They have all gone to the beach," shouted Kawsu, herding small children away from the pool.

"Yes, I know, Kawsu. How are you?"

"Fine, Demba! Are you all right?"

"Yes, fine," I called as I went into the room, changing into swim shorts and grabbing my pack. I took the long way to the beach, walking the road by Bakau's market, past the houses of expats and government officials. Flowers draped their balconies, the pink and orange spreading over the walls, swaying in the wind faster than my feet plodded through the sand. A teenager on a rickety bicycle pedaled past, legs pumping, then stopped and got off his bike.

"Hello," he said, and began to walk beside me. "How is it?"

"No problems," I said. "How is the day?"

"No problems. You have a nice watch. Can you give it to me?"

"My watch? No, sorry, no."

"Oh. Okay," said the boy. After a moment he got back on his bicycle and pedaled off, leaving me alone in the dust.

I was glad to see the ocean glinting beyond the trees,

and hurried to meet the girls who lay sunning themselves on the beach. But there wasn't much conversation there, and I wandered along the waterline, filling my pockets with shells, bending to pick new discoveries from the sand, wading in and out of the charging surf and feeling the water swirl around my feet.

As I walked back to the group, I felt motion on my thigh. Nothing should ever be alive in your pockets, but I put a hand in and something scrabbled against my skin, its tiny claws scratching wildly. Squealing, I flung a handful of shells out onto the sand. A confused-looking hermit crab picked itself up and scuttled away toward the surf, its shell rocking behind it.

"Nnnngh!" I cried, hastily emptying the rest of my pockets. Two more crabs picked themselves up and made for the water. Hesitantly, I inspected the remaining shells, looking for the flap-like cover on the shell's entrance that meant there was a tenant inside. A few looked occupied, and these I put down hastily. The rest I gathered up, making sure to double-check before putting them anywhere near my pants. There were already shells in my backpack, and when I felt inside, more claws scrabbled against my fingers. I shook out the pack, flailing it wildly to make sure no surprises remained, not wanting anything to crawl up my arm in the middle of the night. I do not do well with chitinous things.

As I climbed the stairs to my room that night, a wedding was in full swing down below, lights shining on women in bright dresses, men in dark suits and long white robes. The heavy beat of hip-hop and deep, drumming music rose from the ground, vibrating in my bones. Wild calls and ululations broke the music, the joyful energy unmistakable.

"This is the life," I thought, collapsing facedown into bed, unable to roll over and hoping I wouldn't smother in my sleep.

• • •

The next day was laundry day. Huge, thick-armed women did the hotel's laundry in a small, steam-filled shack behind the dining hall, beating linens and throwing them into washing machines with angry force. They charged a few dalasi for each piece when we wanted our clothes washed, and took their time finishing.

Outside the sun shone, the cerulean sky blotted only by faint wisps of puffy clouds. It was perfect weather for a day at the sea, and that was where I wanted to be, but Zach and I both had a habit of waiting till we had no more clean clothes before we surrendered our dirty ones.

When the bossy lady in charge of the laundry finally returned our clothes, we left for Leybato. We'd barely passed the mosque before Zach remembered he needed to write home, waved goodbye, and disappeared into the Sweet Planet Café. His fiancée worried about him if he didn't send word regularly.

On the corner, taxis idled on their way toward Timbooktoo, the drivers leaning out the window to see if anyone wanted a ride. A woman jumped in front of me and claimed the first car that came along, but I was ready as the second rattled toward me, my arm raised to flag him down.

"You go to Leybato?" I said, sticking my head in the window.

"Leybato? How much?"

"Five dalasi," I said, quoting the price Debbie gave me when I asked how much a taxi cost.

"Five dalasi?" scoffed the man. "No, no, thirty."

"Thirty? No, five. Maybe ten."

"You pay twenty," he said, beginning to rev his engine.

"Twenty? C'mon, that's not the real price!"

"Yes, twenty real price," he said, speeding away. "This taxi!"

"I know it's 'taxi,'" I shouted after him. "That's what I

want to take!"

This transport business still took some getting used to, and it wasn't helped by the fact that despite the lines I've drawn in this book, everyone called everything "taxi." They might occasionally say "tourist taxi" or "town taxi," but this was usually just to clarify it for *tubabs*, after it became clear they didn't know what they wanted. Usually people just said, "You want to take taxi?" which meant, "Do you want a ride instead of walking to Banjul?" This was almost always rhetorical, almost always asked on the way to the taxi park, and only after I became familiar with the system did I know which type of ride they meant.

The next driver had the same reaction, shaking his head and speeding off, leaving me standing flabbergasted in a cloud of blue smoke. After the third driver laughed in my face and sped away, I began to think there was a trick to this. Perhaps if I flirted with them. That usually worked for the girls.

Later I realized that when Debbie told me the price for a taxi, she quoted town taxi prices, and that was what I offered to the men in the yellow cabs. But in the meantime I ambled down the street, ignorant of my sin as I passed barbershops painted with pictures of the hairstyles you could find inside. I wasn't crazy enough to see if they could give me a "7-Up," a "Fresh Prince," or a "Boeing 707," so I kept walking until I reached the beach and sat in the shade of a restaurant with Mary, Debbie, and Aurore. Mary was taking care not to lie out on the beach too much; with her red hair and fair skin, she didn't look like she got along with the sun.

"You're looking a little burned there," I said, noting how pink she'd turned.

"My skin turned green one time," she said, "and my mother's had sun poisoning."

"And you came to Africa?"

Mary smiled, as if to say we were all crazy, and I couldn't help but smile back. We stayed at the beach as long as we could, but the day was over before we knew it. The sun set in the sky, and trudging away from the beach, I kept thinking that all good things must come to an end.

• • •

"Demba Ceesay!" cried Baie the next day, in a high state of excitement when I strolled into the National Museum. "We heard yesterday from the ministry — the Ministry of Culture and Tourism. They accepted our proposal for a training center! We will build it in Brikama."

He showed me the equipment catalog he'd ordered from Italy, flipping through pages of presses, lathes, and cutting machines, peering at the pictures and holding the catalog like a precious treasure.

"I want to get a wire roller," he said, "and we can get an electronic scale. We have one from the post office but it is broken, so we use this," and he pulled out an old balance scale, putting a brass weight in one pan, adding scraps of metal to the other side until they were equal. I snapped a photo, and Samba leaned in to watch, looking with obvious interest at the pictures I took.

Baie showed me some of the work he did, the fine filigree pieces for a bracelet, a cutout of Africa, and a *ju-ju* on a silver chain. "This would be easier with the machines," he said, pointing to the finely twisted filigree wire. "My father would put a piece of cloth through a loop in the end of the wire, turning it over and over so that it became thin. Now I use a piece of wood to turn it, but it is still hard. With a machine it would be much better." He fell silent, gazing at the catalog again in delight, his fingers tracing the shapes of the machines.

For a long time I'd remained fixated on the idea that the old and the new would be separate when I looked at crafts, still getting used to the idea that in the Gambia the two might not be. Seeing Baie's enthusiasm about the tools he would be able to buy, I realized that it worked both ways. If the ancient could still exist with the new, the modern could intrude on the old, and maybe the things I saw along the coast were as "real" as the Africa upcountry.

Baie's son Jambo came into the workshop just then, having finished with his chores. He'd been sweeping the ground outside.

"Because you must be obedient," said Baie, shaking his finger at me and calling Jambo over.

"I come here," said Jambo, "now that I have finished my grade twelve courses."

"I am trying to see if Jambo can go to college in America," said Baie, who knew my father was a university professor. "He is very good at sports. Maybe your father can talk to someone?"

"I like basketball," chimed in Jambo.

"Maybe I can talk to my father," I said, unsure it would help but willing to try. "You know, my dad's college is sometimes big in basketball, but that is mostly the women's team."

"He is very good," repeated Baie, and I promised to ask my father.

The sun reached its zenith as I sat and watched Baie twist copper and silver wires, turning them over and over to wrap the two together. He hammered the wires until they molded into one ring, a two-colored snake that he threw into a basin of clear liquid.

"It is water mixed with hydrochloric acid," he said as the metal fizzled. Using tongs, he pulled the ring from the mixture and rubbed it dry, showing me the metal polished to a high sheen.

"Here," he said, holding it out to me. "You take it!"

At lunchtime the men bought a pot of spicy *benachin*, a rice dish made with habanero peppers, and we ate from a communal bowl, hunched around it in the shade of the neem trees. I was pleased they invited me to eat with them, and they seemed pleased that I accepted.

"Demba," said Baie, "you like *benachin*? It's good?"

"Yes, Baie. It's good!" Samba, Jaja, and Baie laughed at this. I smiled and shoveled another spoonful of rice into my mouth, more than happy to be there.

When we couldn't eat any more and set down our spoons, Samba filled a small kettle with tea, balancing it carefully on the glowing embers of the forge before he set about washing the filthy glasses that were always strewn around the tiny shop. We sat and drank *ataaya*, laughing and smiling in the shade and golden sun of afternoon, while the glass singed my fingers and I sipped the scalding drink slowly, sucking air to cool my tongue. *Ataaya* is traditionally served three times — the first glass as bitter as life, the second as strong as love, and the third as gentle as death, or something like that, and it's rude to leave before drinking all three, so I stayed in their happy company for several hours, drinking to life, love, and death. But finally it was time to go home, and across the street the car park filled with vans, people loading their bags onto them in great piles.

"Bakau?" I called, going from car to car. "Bakau?"

A man in a pair of ragged old shorts pointed me to a beat-up van half-full of passengers, and I sat down behind a white man in a sweat-stained shirt, an Australian bush hat clamped down on his head above a ponytail and wild bushy beard. Next to him, a fat woman wearing a polka dot dress held a live chicken in her lap.

The van filled quickly, and the driver climbed in, his assistant pulling the door shut as we rumbled over the curb and into traffic. He had to hold the door shut, because it threatened to slide open with every bump we hit, but with his free hand the tout began collecting fares, and I felt a sudden burst of pride as I handed over five dalasi, taking a bush taxi by myself.

"This is much easier than regular taxis," I thought as we passed over the bridge in the marshes. There were fixed routes, regular fares, and best of all, no debating with the driver while standing like a fool on the side of the road.

• • •

The next day broke cool and cloudy, the sky painted over with gray. Mighty and I stood on the side of the road, watching bush taxis rush past until one came along with a man leaning out the window shouting "Banjul, Banjul." In Albert Market, we searched for fish bones at the stalls where hawkers bought raw materials for their goods and piles of tiny vertebrae spilled out of ratty cardboard boxes. They didn't cost much, but Mighty kept trying to find better deals, going from one stall to the next. Fishing line and screw clasps took a bit more finding, but we needed them for what I wanted. I'd seen Mighty making necklaces, stringing together long lines of white fish bones and small wooden beads, and I wanted to do the same.

All around the paths hemmed us in, crowded with men in long robes and small boys who ran about, women and girls following behind. Occasionally we came to an open area ringed by carpenters sanding new furniture, women selling fresh fruit, or boys selling socks. I dodged a pig, stepping aside as the squealing thing ran around my legs and disappeared down a path. The market sprawled, and I quickly became lost in the twisting maze.

At dinnertime I went down the street from the hotel, slipping into the velvet twilight and sitting with Gambians at the Rhun Palm as music videos played on the tiny television. In the early days of our research projects, I'd eaten my meals at McFaddy's, an unfortunately named fast food joint near the embassy. It was familiar, a retreat from rice and peanut sauce, a place to spot Peace Corps volunteers and the occasional sweat-stained expatriate wolfing down a burger. But now I'd largely abandoned McFaddy's in favor of the Rhun Palm, and I was hungry enough to order two plates of the spiciest *benachin* I'd ever eaten. It felt like they'd taken hot peppers and used the other ingredients as a garnish. I gave up after one plate, and decided to eat a candy bar from the local "white man's store." The next few minutes proved interesting, as my stomach erupted and made it clear, in no uncertain terms, that spice and chocolate don't mix.

Bakary and I drove south toward Tanje early the following morning. The sun shone overhead, and Aggi was the only craftsmen there when we arrived, standing alone at his forge.

"The name of Kanteh," said Aggi, looking at the forge. "When you see a man with that name, people will know that is a smith."

Bakary nodded. "Whenever we hear it," he said, "even under changed social circumstances, we know that originally they were smiths."

Aggi stoked the fire and pumped the bellows, his hands winnowing the goatskin bags back and forth, stopping occasionally to prod the coals or splash water over the bellows to keep them soft.

"My mother did the bellows when Modou and I were young," said Aggi. "She came from the Damba people. They are also smiths. The women make pots and sell them. It is like that for many blacksmiths."

A small fire burned in the forest behind the museum, its smoke drifting up to the blue-gray sky, and Aggi rose to check on the fire, pouring water over it to make charcoal from the blackened wood.

"You have to watch it," he said, toeing the embers. "You have to observe it."

He showed me a broken hoe that a farmer wanted him to fix, and said there was still some income in the trade, from odd jobs in village to the trinkets and baubles he sold to tourists. But many were learning other trades, finding jobs more profitable than competing with mass production, and he lamented that ever since some of his tools were stolen from the workshop, he didn't have as much equipment as Modou. They'd been stolen five years before, but Aggi still didn't have the money to replace them.

How different our lives were. Aggi was the same age as me, but he had never gone to school, never seen a need for it, and I'd spent most of my life in a classroom. After his father died, Aggi spent his days helping his brother at the forge — the apprentice at the bellows and the master at the anvil. He spoke very little English, and our conversation moved slowly. Every time I asked a question, I was grateful to Bakary for his help. He had done so much already, helping me as I attempted to make connections in the Gambian craft community, and now he translated my questions. Bakary was what every anthropologist dreams of: a knowledgeable informant who could introduce a researcher to the people he wanted to study. Sitting on rough logs, we spent hours learning about the blacksmith's life, and by the time we climbed into Bakary's old Mercedes, weariness crept over me.

Before we went far, Bakary pulled off the road into Tanje fishing village. Oily smoke filled the air, thick with the pungent odor of fish caught by the fishing fleet that bobbed offshore, the worn pirogues slipping in and out of sparkling waves. Sea gulls whirled above us, screeching their raucous cries over fishing nets and boats drawn up on the beach for a new coat of paint. Men relaxed in the shade of metal shacks, watching the work of the men painting, but roused when Bakary asked to buy fish. Soon the stench of the day's catch filled the car, leaving a trail of fumes behind us as we drove north toward the Friendship with the sun glinting on the blacktop.

The other students lounged around the hotel when I returned, resting from their daily expeditions. Left to our own devices, we no longer ate every meal in the quiet of the hotel dining room, or saw each other every day, but we still spent some days in the shade of the pool bar, playing cards and trading stories about the Gambians we'd met as the cook made delicious pies, stuffed with meat and fish, that I ate four at a time. Some nights we went to Senegambia, or Fajara, eating more rice and spicy chicken than was healthy. Sometimes we went to the tiny cement closets that lined the dirt streets, ordering egg sandwiches and warm Cokes from owners who inevitably turned out to be mustachioed Lebanese men, the Lebanese having moved in and taken over local businesses some years before.

But more and more we ate with our Gambian friends, filling ourselves with *benachin* and *yaasa*, wandering in and out, going our own ways and working on our projects. Casey interviewed women about polygamy, Abby spent her days at Katchikally, Zach and Christina disappeared upcountry each week, returning on the weekends to show us redder sunburns. Everyone learned something, and tried to make the most of the time we had left.

A man named Boubacar worked at the hotel pool, cleaning it whenever the fancy struck him, but in his ample spare time he sold tie-dye sheets, bead rings, and other bright trinkets to the tourists at the hotel. We were eager customers, and it looked like we'd made an effort to assimilate, if only in the most superficial fashion. All the girls had their hair done up in cornrows by women who almost pulled it out by the roots, my luggage filled with clothes, and as I walked toward Kairaba Avenue that afternoon, the Gambian colors of a new ring on my finger made me feel right at home.

It seemed silly to dress in the wild fabric of a country that had been foreign to me a month before. I had a slight tan going, but at the current rate it would take me several millennia to fit in, and no one would ever mistake me for a Gambian. I could learn every language the locals spoke, decipher every one of their customs, and wear a *boubou*, but if I went into a strange village they would still call me *tubab*. As if to illustrate the point, a group of children ran toward me on Kairaba, calling *"Tubab, tubab,"* and holding their hands out for pens as I slipped into the cool of an Internet café.

"You want to use Internet?" said the man behind the counter. "No, sorry. The server is down."

"No Internet?" I asked in consternation, and when the man shook his head I turned and went back out in the hot air, my feet turning of their own accord toward McFaddy's, where I ordered a burger and sat down to think.

"This won't do at all," I thought, chewing half-heartedly on the burger. This was a curious trait of the Gambia, and one of the hardest things to get used to: the fact that on any given occasion, there was a decent chance that something wouldn't work when you showed up. It made certain things maddeningly difficult.

The restaurant was almost empty, save for a pair of *tubabs* and me. We ate in silence, watching each other surreptitiously, and as I ate I wondered what movie would be playing at the local cinema — the American embassy, which hosted weekly movie nights. I decided to check it out. It took some time to get inside, because there was procedure to follow as I emptied my pockets, went through the metal detector, went through again because my belt set the detector off, and held my pants up with one hand as I went through for the third time because I'd lost five pounds since arriving in the Gambia.

Long shadows fell across the courtyard by the time I opened a door to the embassy's cool interior, saying a silent prayer for air conditioning before I sat down in the room where we'd had our briefing weeks before. I made a mental checklist of the things I'd done that I wasn't supposed to. Drinking the water? Check. Wandered around alone at night? Not yet. Gotten drunk and made a fool of myself? There was still time. I felt out of place in my none-too-clean t-shirt, measured against the collared shirts of the young men and women filtering into the room, and realized I was more used to hanging around with strange Africans than strange *tubabs*. But they were friendly enough, and soon some of the girls joined me, and I sat in awe at the wonder of moving pictures, even as the power went off three times, leaving us in darkness and reminding us we weren't in America anymore.

When the movie ended, I wandered off alone into the night. The embassy's safety talk, so carefully designed to keep us from doing just that, had clearly failed. I faded into the gloom, picking my way among the trash of the back streets. Halfway home I realized how stupid it might be. In the darkness, strange voices called and shadowy figures beckoned. I hurried past, stumbling, suddenly nervous to be alone, making my way through the pitch until I saw the comforting lights of the Friendship shining over the compound wall. Sighing with relief, I waved at the welcome guards before climbing the stairs to bed.

## CHAPTER THIRTEEN
# Side Effects May Include

Rainstorms swept through Bakau as we slipped into the last two weeks of the trip, battering the hotel courtyard and making us run for cover. The land grew green, if not lush, and though the mosquitoes loved it, they still didn't venture up to the third story, preferring to lie in wait and pounce whenever Zach and I joined the others for dinner.

I did almost nothing the day after Bakary and I went to Tanje, spending the daylight hours by the pool and the evening in my room, listening to another wedding take place downstairs. The lights were on, African music beat, and the women's dresses swirled by the pool bar. I felt the bass in my bones, pounding, thumping, vibrating through the walls and making sleep impossible as the music continued into the night. I lay awake listening, looking up at the mosquito net hanging above my bed, feeling the beat and wondering if I would ever make sense of this place.

There were worse ways to relax, but the next day I was restless and rose early. I felt tired, but it was a good kind of tired, the weariness of long days and time in the sun.

"You are ready to see my friend?" said Mighty, waiting for me downstairs and dressed in a light blue robe — his Friday best — for the Muslim prayers that afternoon. He'd promised to introduce me to a silversmith in Senegambia, and he prayed before we left, kneeling on a mat and facing east toward Mecca as he bowed to Allah. When he finished, another man took his place, the sound of his prayers echoing behind us.

We found the smith's shop on a dirt street not far from the Senegambia craft market. A sign above the door read "Dawda & Gibril, Qualified Gold & Silversmiths."

"*Salaam aaleekum*," said Mighty as he entered.

"*Salaam aaleekum*," I echoed.

"*Maleekum salaam*," replied the men who sat inside, working behind a display case filled with jewelry. The work in the case was beautiful, fine filigree bangles and delicate silver pendants with *ju-jus* and elephants on the chains. The youngest of the men rose and introduced himself as Modou Secka.

"This is my brother Gibril," said Modou, pointing to an older man with a wiry frame. "He is the boss here." The hands of the men behind the counter blurred, and the ring of hammer blows made a constant din over our voices.

"When you say he is your 'brother' what do you mean?" I had to ask, because "brother" could mean "the son of my parents" or "cousin" or "friend."

"His uncle is my father," explained Modou. Everyone at the shop was related to each other and to Baie Mbowe, driving home the point that Gambian crafts were a family business. But even with the close family relations, the men agreed that endogamy — the practice of marrying within a group — was fading.

"Now you can marry whoever," said Modou. "Before it was the daughter of your mother's brother. Now it is anyone, even someone who is not in a silversmith family."

Outside, crucibles the size of shot glasses littered the edge of a tiny forge, and in its center black coals smoked, hissing faintly, the bellows blowing air as Modou went to work on a ring, fanning the coals until flames leaped up.

"You have to be careful," said Modou, turning the

crank on the bellows. "Some people will try to cheat you. They will try to sell you a bangle made of silver and say it is gold. There is a black stone we use to test." He took out a fist-sized lump of rock. "You scratch the metal on it. If it turns red it is copper. Silver will leave a white mark on the stone. For gold you have to put acid on the stone to tell the purity. The higher the purity, the brighter the mark will be."

Gibril was doing pull-ups from the doorframe when we went back in, and the biceps in his skinny arms bulged, attesting to long hours spent hammering. Certificates and pictures of holy men decorated the walls, and Modou showed off a photo of an older man accepting an award from Jammeh.

"That is Dawda," said Modou, "our uncle, who owns the shop. He is the manager of the GGSSA. Gibril is the technical director, and Jaja," meaning Jaja Touray of the Banjul silversmiths, "is the treasurer." Modou and Gibril had been members of the GGSSA for years, and agreed it was time to change some traditions, time to teach outsiders the craft, not just family.

"Like the training center," said Gibril. "I will be a teacher there when it opens. I like to teach others, because what I know in my head about this profession is too much."

"It is still a good job," said Modou, who was young enough not to have children yet. "If I have sons I will teach them."

At lunchtime, Modou put a teapot on the forge and we drank *ataaya*, sweating in the heat. Afterward I walked to the craft market across the road, wondering where I could find the factories that churned out so many necklaces and bracelets. Everything in the stalls looked the same, but that didn't stem my desire to buy everything in sight, going from stall to stall until I saw a beautiful necklace of polished bone. I hadn't learned the trick of feigning indifference, and the man behind the stall saw the gleam in my eye. I wanted that necklace, and he knew it.

"One hundred twenty," he said when I asked.

"No, give it to me for sixty dalasi," I said. "I pay that much for two necklaces somewhere else." This was a silly thing to argue about, but there I was, bargaining over two dollars. I'd turned into one of those tourists, the ones nobody wants to associate with, the ones who give other travelers a bad name.

"No, this is cow bone," he said, holding it up and showing it to me.

"Even for cow bone, I pay less."

He sneered. "You pay less? I don't think so."

"Come on, give me good price." My voice turned into a desperate whine. Bargaining broke down quickly if one party refused to play along, and I felt like we weren't getting anywhere. I was angry he hadn't lowered the price, and began to lose my patience. I also thought about paying whatever he wanted, but Mighty grabbed my arm when I reached for my wallet.

"Let's go," he muttered. "This man, he is no good."

"You, why you want to help him?" demanded the man. He spat an unintelligible curse at Mighty, and Mighty shouted something back, pulling me away.

"What did he say?" I asked when we were out of earshot.

"He said, 'You are the white man's bitch.' There are always people like that. If they see a white man they will not offer the good price, and they won't bargain because they know you have money. They do not want to be your friend; they just want to take your money."

We caught a taxi on the corner, and as it pulled out I was glad, not for the first time and not for the last, that Mighty was my friend. I wanted to buy him a beer, but when the car dropped me in front of the Friendship, I realized I had to use the bathroom with some urgency. I rushed to the room, threw open the bathroom door, and stopped short as my horrified eyes saw an empty toilet paper roll.

"We're out of toilet paper." Zach's voice came from the bed where he sat Indian-style, engrossed in his computer.

"Well, yes, I can see that. Why didn't you get more?"

He shrugged. "Well, I didn't have to go."

"Dammit, Zach," I cursed, sprinting for the reception desk. There was no one behind it, and I rang the bell frantically, trying to make it as loud as Notre Dame. At last a man appeared from a back room and looked at me blankly when I asked for toilet paper. Immediately, if it wasn't too much to ask. He gave a put-upon sigh, retreated to the room he'd come from, and returned holding a roll. It could have been the Holy Grail, I grabbed it so fast, and by taking the stairs four at a time I managed to make it to the bathroom. After that I stockpiled toilet paper.

As darkness fell Chef Szo prepared a feast for us on the hotel lawn: chicken, fish, deviled eggs, and tiny pink prawns. I fell in love with everything except the prawns, which stared at me with beady black eyes, and it was hard to dissociate the desiccated, smelly market fish from the meal we were eating. Somewhere between there and the dining table, the fish had been transformed from rotting things to tender delicacies, but they were still full of bones, and I coughed, catching one in my throat.

A troupe of Gambian women danced on the lawn, all broad shoulders and glowing skin, waving their hips, their figures outlined by bright skirts and white bras, colorful head wraps above bare shoulders. The women brought a mortar with them and pounded a pestle into it, the blows sounding deeply as they stomped the ground. Soon they called for everyone to dance, but I begged off, still busy eating everything in sight. The others joined and danced back and forth, their faces orange from the lights, smiling, happy faces shining in the night. There are few things funnier than full-grown adults hopping around like chickens.

I wished we could be together like this every night, and didn't want it to end. But eventually everyone drifted off, and I climbed the stairs to one of the rooms, crowding in with the others to watch a movie. Our heads nodded wearily in its flickering light, and half-sleeping figures slumped everywhere. It was after midnight when I dragged myself to bed, tired at last, leaving the world outside quiet and still.

• • •

I regarded the alarm clock with a mixture of confusion and annoyance when it rang the following morning. It was going off, that much was clear, but what did it mean? I considered it a small accomplishment that I could recognize the source of the sound at all, thinking that more than one morning had come and gone without me realizing what made that annoying sound.

Suddenly I remembered I needed to meet with Fatty, and should be getting up soon if I wanted to make it on time. I groaned, too tired to do anything other than smack the alarm clock off the nightstand and hope it would hit the snooze button on its way down.

I had a few more minutes of sleep before the door banged open and Zach walked in, his entrance heralded by the sound of drums. The Roots festival had begun, and booming announcements echoed from Independence Stadium, where all the girls had gone to watch the opening ceremony.

"Weren't you supposed to go talk to a guy today?" said Zach. He was back from upcountry and engaged in his full-time leisure activity of giving me grief.

"I didn't feel like it," I groaned from the bed, pulling the sheet up over my head.

"You lazy bastard."

I used the only retort I could think of and told him to

shut up. I needed breakfast before I could debate in a civilized manner, but it was pointless anyway. I was already late, and once I'm late I figure it's easiest not to show up at all. With no further incentive to head out early, I'd just risen when I heard a bump from the other side of the room, and out of the corner of my eye I saw Zach slide off the bed, knocking things off his bedside table as he went.

"Very funny, Zach," I said, thinking he was playing a joke. But I looked over and he was on the floor, his head thrown back, his arms crossed over his chest, hands curled like claws. White foam covered his mouth.

"Zach!" I yelled, trying to get a response, but there was nothing. He'd told me he was epileptic, but never said how to deal with a situation like this. In lieu of something useful, I decided to panic.

"Oh shit, oh shit, oh shit," I cried, running down to Bill's room and pounding on the door. There was no response. Some of the girls sat in their room a few doors down, and they looked up when I appeared.

"Has anyone seen Bill?" I cried, looking like a disheveled lunatic only half-dressed at ten in the morning. They shook their heads, and I sprinted for the front desk, ringing the bell at a pace generally reserved for machine gun fire until a man appeared and said yes I could use the phone if I would only stop abusing his bell. Fingers shaking, I dialed Bill's number, muttering "Pick up, pick up" all the while.

"Bill," I shouted when he answered. "Zach's having a seizure, and I don't know what to do!"

"Well, make sure he doesn't swallow his tongue." Bill sounded as if he were reading from a long and slightly boring sermon.

"How am I supposed to do that?"

"Just check his mouth. I'll be there soon." Click. The phone went dead. I sprinted back, taking the stairs four at a time and nearly bowling over a Gambian coming out of the room. Ami and a young man crouched over Zach, who still lay where he fell.

"Here, help me get him onto the bed," said the man. He grabbed Zach's legs, I grabbed his arms, and we heaved him onto the bed. He was stiff, but his arms no longer clutched his chest like a corpse's. I tried checking his mouth, but his jaw felt wired shut, his teeth clenched together. The girls gathered outside, hovering hesitantly by the door with worried eyes, and I could only think, "Dammit, Zach, don't die on me."

A groan escaped his lips, and I saw movement. He recovered gradually, like a man coming up from a deep and distressing dream, progressing from complete unawareness to garbled mumbling and finally to full responsiveness. By the time Bill arrived he was even talking, although the first things out of his mouth didn't make much sense, and aside from a bump on the head and some scratches where his fingernails dug into his arms, he seemed fine.

We spent the rest of the day at the hotel as he recovered. Zach had no memory of the event — certainly it was more memorable for the rest of us — and didn't believe me when I told him he slid out of bed like a drunk.

"I really had a seizure?"

I nodded. "You really did."

"Although…" He thought about it. "The first time I had a seizure I blacked out in class and woke up with people standing over me looking concerned."

"That sounds about right."

"I wonder if it had anything to do with the stuff I'm taking for malaria."

"Are you taking mefloquine?" I asked, rummaging through my bag and pulling out the bottle of malaria medication. The doc had warned me that mefloquine might have side effects for epileptics.

"No, I'm taking Lariam," said Zach.

"Those are the same things," I sighed, holding up the bottle and reading where the warning label said, "MAY CAUSE SEIZURES."

## CHAPTER FOURTEEN
# Serrekunda, Serrekunda!

I arrived at the beach in good time on Sunday, riding in Bill's "shimmy mobile," which in defiance of all natural laws still worked. Somehow it had even improved, and only tried to crash itself twice.

Later, when the sun had burned everyone red, the rest of our group boarded a bus to follow the Roots festival up-country to Kanilai, where the president had invited us to attend a traditional initiation ceremony called a *futampaf*. Only Zach and I stayed in our room as day receded into night and the colors outside turned golden. We both had our reasons. Zach was going to Juffreh-Albreda in the morning, and I had no desire to watch dancing drummers for hours on end. There would probably be speeches about Jammeh's generosity, and an ambassador or two to lend some ostentation to the event. But I was intent on going to Tanje the next day, sleeping soundly until then and eating as much as I could before bed.

In the morning, Mighty and I took a taxi into Serrekunda, the largest collection of ramshackle buildings in the Gambia. It was crowded, incredibly crowded, as if the entire town had come out and decided to pack the streets with honking vehicles. Our van made its way in slowly, the driver using the horn to move us around upturned wheelbarrows, but the town sprawled on, and we wove ever deeper through the broken streets to one of the taxi parks that served as hubs for western Gambia.

The park spread over a dirty brown lot, the potholed ground strewn with piles of things best not considered, and I coughed, almost gagging as I covered my mouth, stepping gingerly among the refuse. Women sold fruits and vegetables on what little ground wasn't covered in foul-smelling gunk, and stalls hawked everything from nuts and bolts to radios, televisions, and machetes. Serrekunda was a market town.

Taxis for common destinations were easy enough to find in Bakau. Vehicles bound for Banjul and Serrekunda drove by every half hour or so, with a tout leaning out the window and yelling the destination. An outstretched hand was all you needed to catch one, but anything beyond that had to be found in a car park and it wasn't always easy to locate the taxi you needed. Mighty and I went from car to car, poking our heads in the windows and saying "Tanje, Tanje" to everyone we met, but it was hard enough to find the drivers of the vehicles. The men knew it might be hours before they had enough passengers to make a trip worthwhile, and many slept in the shade, or sat around small pots of tea, shoulders hunched as they sipped *ataaya*, teeth bared to suck air over scorched tongues.

Finally, we found a car to Gunjur. It wasn't Tanje, but it was on the road we wanted, and we climbed on, peering out at the bustle around us. We still had time to observe the market, because even if we'd found a car, the driver was nowhere in sight. After a while he finally appeared, and slowly the rest of his customers piled into the vehicle, chickens and mangoes on their laps, and we drove south.

Almost two hours after leaving the Friendship, we arrived at the gate to Tanje and stood by the roadside as the van roared off, spewing a cloud of smoke behind it. Tanje is only ten miles on good roads south of Bakau, which gives an idea of how travel works in the Gambia.

"You are here?" exclaimed Mr. Jadama, the assistant, his face screwing up in confusion when we walked in. "You did not go to Kanilai? Mr. Sidibeh called to say you were not going to be able to come, so the weaver has not come in today!" I was sure my face fell, because he immediately added, "But we can call him, and perhaps he will come. And the blacksmith is just arriving."

"So sorry I am late," said Modou, who stood over a half-dozen cases that he and Aggi set up every time they came in, filling them with bangles and necklaces for sale. "I thought you were not coming today." He went into his small shelter and gathered leaves, pushing them into the mouth of the forge. A match flared and he used the dry leaves to start a fire, blowing gently and fanning the flames before adding charcoal.

"It used to be easier to work," said Modou as Mighty translated. "It was easier to find the ironwood tree to make charcoal, and people needed more tools. Now we will repair a tool, but it will last a long time so there is not a big market. People with workshops in town make more money and have machines to help them."

"My older son Ahasana is fifteen. He goes to school in the mornings and comes to work here in the afternoons and weekends. I want my sons to learn the trade, so that my family will not forget smithing, even if they have other jobs." Modou was thirteen when his own father died, leaving the boy only half-trained, but his father had four wives, and Modou learned the rest of the trade from his older half-brothers, who taught him darker secrets along with the tools of the trade.

"There is a special prayer to help farmers before planting," said Modou, showing more enthusiasm than I'd seen all day as he talked about the spells that make blacksmiths powerful figures in traditional life. "Some prayers can heal wounds, or cure the sick. They can even curse people." He looked both ways as he said this, as if revealing it was a transgression, and I leaned in close, intrigued by this sudden turn of events. Now we were getting somewhere.

"There is a vengeful prayer," continued Modou, clearly taking this seriously. "When we use it, it will make a man's private parts big, so big they will be very painful. There is no cure until the blacksmith lifts the curse, so people respect him because of what he can do." He nodded for emphasis, and I grunted in what I hoped was a suitably impressed manner, thinking that there might be some Westerners who would pay good money for that kind of curse.

"Maybe you can give him something?" whispered Mighty when we rose to go. I reached in my pocket and fished out a few bills, wondering if Modou would make my private parts painfully large if I didn't pay him for his time.

By then the weaver had arrived, his young apprentice in tow, and they were readying the loom when I wandered over, the apprentice sweeping the area with a bundle of sticks, tracing long circles in the dirt.

"I moved to Tanje in two t'ousand and one," said Ousman. "I have land here, and I farm it during the rainy season. Traditionally, weaving is a seasonal job, during the dry time when there is cotton to use." His parents were farmers and weavers, and taught him both because education was no guarantee of a job — the same reason he never went to school.

The apprentice stopped sweeping behind us, and while we talked he kept pulling shawls and woven bags out and stringing them up for sale.

"Both bride and groom must wear woven cloth," said Ousman, picking up a long sash of thick cotton. "At christening ceremonies the baby should be wrapped in a woven cloth, and when the boys are circumcised, the circumcision clothing is woven." He reflected for a moment. "But there are very few weavers left. My wife Jainaba is not from a weaving family. She is from a shepherd family. I have one son, Muhamed, who is one year old now. I will teach him weaving if he wants to learn, but I want him to go to school, and choose what he wants to do."

I stayed a while longer, but finally Mighty and I walked to the roadside, waving plaintively at passing bush taxis, though it took some time before we found one going in the right direction. I wouldn't have minded the wait — I wasn't usually in a hurry, Gambian time being what it was — but we wanted to be back at the Friendship to say goodbye to Liza, a graduate student who popped in and out of the *tubab* collection at the hotel. She was leaving, and when Mighty and I made it back from Tanje, we found her with Ellyn, one of the semester students, a blonde girl with a big smile and bright blue eyes.

We hadn't eaten, so Mighty and I went to the Rhun Palm, where the television was dark and the room deserted except for a man who popped out of the kitchen to ask if we wanted the daily meal. Outside a procession marched past, full of men chanting slogans. I asked a man what was going on, and he looked me up and down.

"It is just a small politician," he said. "They are his supporters." We never covered politics in Mandinka, and I couldn't understand a word of the chants. Drums beat, women carried palm fronds, waving them above honking cars, and I spotted a praise-singer — a *griot* — hired to sing the praises of anyone with money to pay his fee.

Mighty and I spent the afternoon making fish bone necklaces with Ellyn, sitting in Liza's room and watching her pack. It's a curious feeling watching someone else pack, with the frantic back-and-forth of trying to fit everything in, especially when in a week or so you'll have to attempt the same thing, and with bags filled to bursting by a growing addiction to African crafts. When it was time to leave we threw her bags into Bill's car and piled in next to the girls, driving through the blazing sun toward Yundum. But at the airport, the news wasn't good.

"What do you *mean*, my flight was canceled?" said Liza. Bill, Ellyn, Mighty, and I hung back from the ticket counter, watching the train wreck of African travel. Liza came out distraught, and we did our best to comfort her, telling her that she could get another flight tomorrow and drown her sorrows tonight.

"If you don't go," said Ellyn, "we can always have beer night at the hotel. I've never had Julbrew." This was why I liked Ellyn. She always looked on the bright side. Julbrew was the local Gambian beer, and one of the most ubiquitous products in the Gambia. Bars that didn't carry much else sold Julbrew, and, inevitably, Coke. It didn't seem right to visit the country without trying at least a sip.

"You've never had Julbrew?" I said, thinking that I'd never had any beer. That settled it, and if we needed an excuse to throw a party, we had one now.

For someone who'd never tried beer, Julbrew was not the appropriate introduction. My first sip that night produced a grimace and the remark that it tasted like shit. The second sip did nothing to improve my opinion, but perhaps I wasn't in a position to judge its merits, given my largely sober history. I don't mean to malign the stout Julbrew, since the other students drank enough of it to drown a camel. Beer is an acquired taste, and what we had here was a failure to appreciate.

Ousman Jallow, a young man who sold drums under the mango tree out front, sat in a corner helping Isaac tighten the skin on a drum he'd bought. They'd taken a length of cord I'd brought to the Gambia, having no idea what I might need in Africa, and Ousman clenched the drum between his feet, pulling the cord tight.

"That's great," said Isaac, who'd bought the drum from

Ousman a few days earlier, the latest victim of a marketing campaign that targeted all the *tubabs* in the hotel. Someone put an old tape in a scratchy boom box, and as we put the drum away, Mighty began dancing around the room to Lynyrd Skynyrd's "Simple Man."

"This is my favorite song," he shouted, grinning wildly. "Oh, be a simple kind of man…"

On the balcony outside, the pungent smoke of reefers filled the air. I joined the students looking out at the darkened compound, but hesitated when they passed the joint my way. I'd never smoked pot, having been less than adventurous in my recreational drug use. I was more tempted than I'd ever been, and the Gambia seemed like a good place to try new things, but ultimately I refrained, not feeling the moment and understanding that "feeling it" was essential to the drug experience. The Gambia opened me up to some new experiences, but not all of them.

The music faded as we sat and talked, leaving our voices the only sound in the night. Down below, the moon shone on the hotel yard, deserted and still. It was late when we left, calling goodbye and "see you tomorrow" to each other. I went back to my room, content like I hadn't been in a long time, thinking that any day ending at two in the morning, wandering off from a party in the African night, is a good day in my book.

• • •

The girls returned from the *futampaf* at three in the morning, and any lingering doubts I had about staying behind disappeared with their arrival. It had been more of the same, nothing but sitting in the sun, watching dancer after dancer, musical troupe after musical troupe parade past while ministers gave long-winded speeches.

None of them were conscious when Mighty, Ellyn, and I went with Liza to Yundum, our fingers crossed for luck. This time there were no surprises at the ticket counter, and soon Liza was on her flight to Dakar. I was sorry to see her go, even if I'd only known her a few days. Friendship seemed like something to cherish here, in the fleeting time we had left. But I suppose friendship is always something to cherish, and sometimes we simply forget. It was good to be reminded.

Mighty and I stopped at St. Mary's on the way back, digging in the freezer for ice cream. St Mary's was a Western supermarket in miniature on Kairaba, with American brands and a wall devoted to liquor, where we retreated when we needed another kind of reminder, a reminder of the comforts of home. The ice cream was for Ellyn. She would leave with Becky and Isaac the next day, and we'd decided to drown our sorrows again that night.

In the afternoon I went back to Kairaba, intent on finding a bottle of rum, walking past children playing soccer in a field behind the Friendship, their feet throwing up puffs of dirt as they ran back and forth. Someone had painted black lines on the dirt a few days earlier, and the lines were already scuffed by heavy use. I heard the familiar call of "*Tubab, tubab*" rising to greet me, and wished Zach was there. When he and I walked into town together, the children bothered Zach more than me, coming up to ask him for "Pen, any pen." He acted like a magnet for every child in the area, and as long as they saw him they left me alone. But now I was without my human shield, and the children stopped playing long enough to run after me calling "*Tubab, tubab!*"

I was sweating by the time I got back to the room, a bottle of Captain Morgan's rum in hand. I'd searched high and low for the Captain, because I consider myself a pirate, and pirates drink Captain Morgan. I was a victim of insidious advertising. St. Mary's didn't have it, much to my surprise, and I headed across the street to another store, ducking into its darkened interior as the electricity failed again.

Finding the rum was the type of dilemma I imagine expatriates deal with on a daily basis, which might explain why they gain a certain reputation for drinking too much.

Despite my dehydration, I immediately opened the bottle and took a swig. I gasped, coughing. It tasted exactly the way I imagine cleaning fluid tastes. I took a second sip, more judicious this time, but it was definitely cleaning fluid. That wasn't a bad thing. In fact, it was just the flavor I wanted. It had the familiar kick of zoom-zoom, the fiery burning in my stomach, and I put it in front of the air conditioner to cool off.

"Is there a reason why there's a bottle of rum in front of the air conditioner?" said Zach when he walked in some time later.

"To cool it," I said, as if that should be obvious.

"I see. Going to have a party later?"

"Cocktail night, baby!"

"I see," he laughed. "Want to go to St. Mary's?"

The calls of "*Tubab*" began again as a group of school-children — no doubt on their way to the hotel pool — stopped to ask for pens. This time all the attention went to Zach. The children clustered around him and left me alone as I stood by, trying not to laugh.

"God dammit," he grumbled, disentangling himself at last. "No wonder no one bothers *you*. You look like a Peace Corps volunteer."

I looked down at my sandals, khaki shorts and plain t-shirt, felt my lengthening hair and unshaven face, and had to admit I did. Peace Corps volunteers were known as the poorest Americans around, and they had a certain look. It didn't stop people from asking for money, but it helped.

"Dammit," I retorted, looking at the Hawaiian shirt he wore. "No wonder the kids beg *you* for money. You look like a tourist."

"God, you're an ass."

"Shut up, tourist-boy!"

"You dirty hippie!"

We were good friends by now, despite the acrimony in our conversation. Together with the others we'd christened our group the Fam in the Gam, and sometimes it surprised me how quickly I'd begun to look on these former strangers as family. Zach and I were brothers, which explained why we argued so much, and we had a host of new sisters, whom we generally acted much nicer to. Abby was the patient one, who watched out for us as we acted like scamps. Amanda was our "Gambian sister" whether she liked it or not, especially when she went to the beach and attracted a crowd of Gambian men, who still didn't know what to make of her. Even Debbie, who was older than us, and a teacher to boot, seemed more like a sister than a professor. Finally, there was Bill, who had slipped into a father-figure role, the man in charge and the answer to all things Gambian.

As night fell we left for dinner, flagging down the first van that came along. A moment of bargaining had us all aboard, and the van rattled to a start, lurching into the dark streets.

"Do you know Luigi's?" asked Debbie, sitting up front with the driver. We drove toward Senegambia, one of the more happening neighborhoods in the Gambia, and the night grew noisier as nightclubs poured out their music, their doors open to reveal young Gambians gyrating to American pop and African reggae. We ate Italian food at a restaurant looking out on the scene, and the pizza seemed like the best I'd ever had. Maybe it was the laughter or the company of friends that made it so good, but whatever the reason, I couldn't imagine being anywhere else.

My feet dragged by the time we returned to the hotel, but the night wasn't over. A cluster of revelers stood on the walkway upstairs, and with rum in hand I ambled to the "kitchen," the room where one of the semester students kept a fridge for emergencies like this.

"So you're a liquor man," said Abby, smelling my drink from across the room. I'd emptied half a bottle of pineapple juice, filled it back up with rum, and now the small room contorted, already full of the last semester students — Becky, Isaac, and Ellyn — and more than a few Gambians who'd wandered in from their hotel rooms. We danced and sang into the night, but the party ended far too early as people drifted off, receding into the darkness. "This isn't how it's supposed to work," I thought, feeling that something must be amiss if I was one of the last to leave a party. Then I looked up and it was only Isaac, Mighty, and me, becoming drunkenly sentimental as we swapped stories outside the "kitchen" door.

Down below, the pool shone under a silvery moon. Thinking there was no better time than two in the morning for a swim, Isaac and I dove into the water. It felt cool and refreshing, a tonic for my drunken brow, and Mighty sat on the pool's edge, smoking something foul as Isaac and I climbed out and dove in again and again. The hotel grew quiet around us, the other guests fast asleep, and drunkenly I spun in the water, making myself dizzy until Isaac and Mighty disappeared and I was alone, spinning in place, suspended in the moonlight.

It wasn't until the next morning that we noticed the dirty cloud in the water, and discovered the filter had broken the week before. A thin film coated the pool, but I didn't have long to worry about it, and only hoped I wouldn't repeat my upcountry experience as I headed out to catch a taxi into Banjul. I had more interviews to conduct, and when I got back Zach and I ended June in our room, packing for a trip to Senegal. We planned to take the morning ferry with the rest and drive north to Dakar the next day, spending a few days and returning by the weekend if all went well. But this was African transport we were dealing with. Murphy's Law is multiplied in Africa, where it's safe to assume that not only will something go wrong, but that everything will go wrong.

We'd almost finished packing when I heard a knock at the door, opened it, and found Christina standing there, grinning with the manic look of someone who's about to deliver bad news.

"The ferry's broken," she said. "Bill says we won't be leaving till Friday." It was Wednesday now, and I sighed, thanking Christina for the news.

"Don't bother packing," I said as I went back into the room, and I heard Zach curse from the bed where he sat with his half-packed bag.

"At least we get to sleep in," I muttered, intending to do just that.

# CHAPTER FIFTEEN
# La Isle Gorée

The sound of Bill pounding on the door, shouting it was time to go, rudely woke me the next morning. They'd fixed the ferry in the night, and after some hasty last-minute packing we arrived at the ferry port to find a long line of vehicles ahead of us. Everyone groaned, sure it would be hours before we even saw the water.

"Excuse me," said Bill, leaning out the window and waving to a policeman guarding the line. "What's your supervisor's name? Can I get his number? Tell him to expect a call from the president's office." Bill took out his phone and began dialing.

"Hello, Mr. So-and-so," said Bill, talking to someone high in the government. "It's Bill. Listen, we're here at the ferry, but we're stuck at the back of the line, and we're running late. I was wondering if you could do something about that. I have the number of the supervisor here at the ferry…"

We looked at each other. Was Bill really calling some minister to bump us to the front of the line? Should we feel bad about this?

I would have, but I had no desire to wait for hours in the heat, and my conscience is a pragmatic one. Soon the policeman came back, waving us from the line as more guards cleared a path, directing cars out of the way. We rolled to the front, managed to make the one o'clock ferry, and found ourselves swaying back and forth with the rhythm of the waves.

The trip across the river seemed shorter this time, and before I knew it we pulled off the pier into the dusty shores of Niumi, driving north toward Senegal. The roads proved flat and smooth, and the drive went quickly, but at every stop we made the locals came out, swarming around the van, begging and trying to sell cashews. Some of the girls bought nuts, hoping it would make the hawkers go away, but it only made them more brazen.

Often our driver veered off-road, speeding over coastal salt flats, and I could see other cars making their way across the flats, the trucks and heavily laden vans avoiding potholes on the road. Near the town of Kaolack, where the Saloum River snaked into the dust, huge mounds of salt gleamed by the roadside and dark stick figures climbed over the white hills, pausing to watch us above evaporating ponds glinting in the sun. A huge mosque rose out of the land ahead, dwarfing everything with its soaring minarets, but despite its impressive size, I could see the paint chipping, a reminder that this was still a poor land.

I'd caught only a fleeting glimpse of the Senegalese capital when we flew through it before, a sight of yellow lights shining in the darkness and a few dirty streets in the morning. Up close Dakar proved huge, full of cars and traffic jams. We sat in endless snarls, watching the sunset and creeping closer to the center of the city, listening to a radio station that played American music requested by callers in pidgin French and Wolof, a strange mix of languages that had at least one of us singing off-key at the back of the van.

The streets grew quiet near the sea, swallowed by the city that towered over us, black in its silent intensity. At the deserted docks, a single bulb lit the empty lot where the van left us, waiting as a ferry's shape crept out of the darkness like some great sea beast. There were no automobiles on Gorée Island, the tiny dot in Dakar harbor where we would stay, and after we boarded the ferry chugged slowly toward it, bobbing up and down on the swell, a light rain falling as we looked out at the small fleck of light in the harbor. A red warning buoy floated a little way off, blinking silently to mark the wreck of a British merchant ship sunk during World War II by the Vichy French government of Senegal.

As we glided into the dock I saw the shore lit with streetlamps that revealed old-world facades on colonial buildings. Cobblestones brought us to our hotel, where Liza waited with her boyfriend François. It was good to see she'd made it, and she waved when she saw us again, but we all felt drained from the long trip, and as much as we wanted to stay up and talk, most of us went to our rooms when the greetings ended. Zach, Bill, and I shared a room in the corner of the old colonial building that served as our hotel. The light of streetlamps below pierced its shuttered windows, and I went to the hallway bathroom to fill a bottle from the sink before going to bed, brushing my teeth with water that tasted like chlorine.

"Probably means everything in it is dead," I thought, too tired to worry as I took a swig. Then I retreated to a bed that was wonderfully soft after hours on the road, but despite my weariness it took a long time to fall asleep as the sounds of the ocean breeze mixed with Bill snoring in the next bunk.

• • •

I woke to bright sunshine and the sounds of Gorée coming alive, which mainly consisted of chickens and people shouting in languages I couldn't understand. Slightly disoriented at finding myself in such an archaic place, I looked around. Bill was missing, but Zach still lay facedown on his mattress, snoring gently.

Rolling out of bed, I threw open the shutters, leaning

out the window to catch a glimpse of the glittering water-front and watch people begin their day. Then I remembered the taste of the tap water the night before, and held my bottle up to the light. The water was the color of piss, and when I looked closer, there were distinctly things floating gracefully through the golden liquid — and therefore my intestines.

Bill and Debbie sat at a table downstairs, talking as I joined them for a breakfast of fresh bread. It seemed we ate little else for breakfast, but at least there wasn't any Tang. I'd been drinking Tang for a month, and slumped over it every morning, staring into the glass and trying to figure out how to choke it down. I'd begun to think the orange drink should be listed as cruel and unusual, and that anyone caught serving it in place of real juice should be shot.

Solicitously, or perhaps noting my expression as I glared at the bread, Bill asked how I'd slept.

"Your snoring kept me up," I told him.

"Well, you know you snore, too."

"I do not," I protested. "Do I?"

Abby and Christina joined us, sipping bags of water, still as cautious as the rest when it came to food and drink.

"Maybe you should drink bottled water," said Abby, looking at my bottle and wincing.

"Yeah, that looks nasty," added Christina, peering into the murk.

"If it's going to kill me," I said, "it's already too late. Do you expect me to pay for water?" Six weeks in Africa had done terrible things to my judgment. Put it down to something I ate — or something I drank.

After breakfast, Bill introduced us to our tour guide for the day, a thin, mustachioed man in dark sunglasses and a long white robe, whose name I promptly forgot.

"I am the Lion," he said, so I called him that as he led us up the alley behind the hotel, pointing to a statue of a woman embracing a man with raised arms and broken chains around his wrists. When the Lion said it stood in front of a slave house, where slaves waited before their journey to the new world, I had my doubts. A house on a surf-swept island was an unlikely place to load human cargo, and most slaves left from mainland sources where European merchants could easily collect them.

Still, that had been when Gorée flourished — the time of slaves and colonial rulers. Now the old buildings lined every cobblestone street on the island, and alleyways twisted among shaded courtyards covered in bougainvillea. It looked like a seaside town in the Mediterranean, as if the Africans had been dropped in a European city instead of the other way around, and the impression only grew stronger at the Church of St. Charles, where decadent chandeliers, statues, and icons seemed out of place in the poor and predominantly Muslim Senegal.

"All the things in this church were carried over with the colonists," said the Lion as we climbed to a balcony over the dark wooden pews.

Gorée sloped steeply upward from the beaches, and we followed the Lion along the Rue des Baobabs, a street lined with stocky trees standing at attention, their branches twisted against a pale blue sky. Up on top the wind whipped across the open spaces of the rocky crown, and a man began to pound on a narrow tom-tom, the beat of his drum filling the air. Behind him an anti-slavery monument towered into the sky, a low quarter-sphere of solid cement and a slender sail of honeycombed white, designed by Italian architect Ottavio di Blasi to represent those who'd been forced to sail west with the slavery ships and the people still in Africa — the two groups united yet separate.

Beyond the monument the edge fell away, down to a sea that smashed relentlessly against the dark basalt columns of the cliff. Trash clung to bushes, which in turn clung to the rocks, trying not to fall into the sea. Artist residences hovered over the sea farther out, so fantastic they looked like they belonged in a fantasy realm, tiny round rooms standing guard above crashing surf, painted pink and green and perched on high precipices.

"They tried to build a bridge from here to Dakar," said the Lion, pointing to a string of cement blocks sinking into the depths. "But it did not work." Judging by the state of the blocks, that was an understatement. White surf foamed and surged around them, making me wonder whose idea it was to build a bridge from the high, rocky side of an island.

"You have seen the movie *Guns of Navarone?*" said the Lion. He pointed to the huge guns that rested atop the island, their days of glory long gone, abandoned and left to rust in the sun. "It is a famous American film, and they filmed it here. In the scene when they scale the cliff, that is the cliff right here." In the movie, soldiers stormed a fortress in Nazi-occupied Greece, but I guess the Greeks were busy and couldn't lend their cliffs to the producers. Instead they made do with the Senegalese island topped by its rusting guns, which had only fired once, to sink the British ship in the harbor.

A monkey climbed out of a pit nearby. His tan ears twitched as the girls stroked his fur, and the drummer was still at his post, hands moving on his tom-tom, his dark arms bare and a *ju-ju* around his neck. The homes of more artists dotted the hillside under the guns, the rock honeycombed with galleries of bright paintings, old military storerooms ceded to artists in the hope that Gorée would become an artist's enclave. Now it was hard to take a step without someone trying to sell you something.

Above it all stood the slave monument, breezy and light in the sun, braced against blue sky, but it was hard to associate this place, so full of laughter and gaiety, with the dark horrors of slavery.

We ate lunch by the beach and watched crowds of people take the ferry to the mainland. When the menu arrived I stared at it, wondering why none of the words made sense before remembering I didn't speak French.

"Aurore, what is this?" I said, pointing at an item.

"I think that's liver."

I made a face. "And what is this?"

"That says 'tip not included.'"

"I see. And how do you say 'chicken?'" I asked plaintively.

"*Poulet.*"

When it came, the chicken was delicious. After lunch we went our separate ways, some toward the shops and others down to the beach, and when I ran into the Lion I asked where I could change money. There weren't any banks on Gorée, and I needed more Central African Francs, the currency of Senegal.

"You need CFA?" said the Lion, leading me into a back room near the beach, where a small man lounged on top of a freezer, his feet dangling over the edge.

"You need CFA?" he said, and pulled out a calculator, punching some numbers as I handed him dalasi. Black market moneychangers offered better rates than the banks, and soon Senegalese notes filled my pockets as I walked back to the hotel, just making it before realizing the other students were nowhere to be found. I was late for a trip to the mainland.

"Go! Go!" urged the manager, pointing at his watch as I hurried out to the ferry launch. In a crowd of Senegalese, Bill and the others proved easy to find, pushing aboard with the rest. The radio played American music again when we reached Dakar, and new cars flashed by, fresh from the dealership, making me stare at their spotless paint jobs. I'd been in the Gambia too long, if I thought a shiny taxi was something special.

The moment we got out at a craft market, a thousand voices called for us to come and see. The tourist season had ended months before, and the venders pulled at our arms, dragging us into stalls, one clutching at my elbow and barring the door when I tried to leave his shop. I quickly learned to say *"mille francs,"* shouting "a thousand francs" at anyone who shoved a carving at me. This was not the smartest bargaining technique, but language barriers left little choice. It was shout something, or be mute and shouted at.

Deeper in the market, stalls were filled with leather shoes and snakeskin belts, the scales as colorful as the rainbow, and beyond them men sold silver elephants and bronze lions, rough-cut things with black eyes and sinewy limbs. The vendors here were far more passive, gazing laconically as I returned to the carvings and was swept back into the whirlwind.

"That is the t'inking man," said one man, seeing me looking at a stick-like carving with an empty face resting on an open palm. "You know the T'inker statue? This is the African t'inking man."

"Yes, I know t'e T'inker," I said, unable to help myself. "How much you want for t'ree?" I'd always liked Rodin's statue, so wonderfully pictured over the gates of hell in Dante's *Inferno*, and it was easier to bargain for large purchases.

Dusk approached and we drove out past Dakar's beaches, past promenades still busy with people strolling and hawking goods, or just standing and watching the passersby. Somewhere on the edge of town we found a French restaurant, its lights shining in the darkness near a mangled car wreck, its gutted remains another reminder of Africa. The menu in the restaurant proved just as impenetrable as the one at lunch, and my French bargaining skills were of no use when confronted with the written word. Trying to find something, I sipped at the wines that the others passed around the table, wishing we had cashew wine instead — or better yet, some zoom-zoom.

"Bill, what's 'Chantilly?'" said Holly, peering at the dessert menu.

Bill perked up and looked at me. "Chantilly? Why, Chantilly lace!"

"Chantilly lace and a pretty face," I shouted, breaking into song, "and a pony tail, hanging down, a wiggle in the walk and a giggle in the talk, make the world go round, round, round!" The girls stared, and maybe it was best that there wasn't any zoom-zoom available.

• • •

Finding hot chocolate at breakfast proved infinitely better than an orange powder drink. I sipped and felt sweat on my brow, waiting in the sun as the others stumbled downstairs. We had the universal gait of people unfamiliar with their surroundings, waking and reacquainting ourselves with reality, wondering where we were and what we were doing there. This state isn't easy to obtain without the effects of alcohol, but travel is a strong substitute.

We had the whole day to explore Gorée, and I started it by spending an hour staring out to sea from the cliff tops, smelling the salt air coursing over the dull brown earth and enjoying the view of Dakar across the water. Every so often I heard the call from a mosque, harsh and tinny in the air above the island. It was peaceful up there, almost spiritual, but when I went back down I devoted the rest of the morning to shopping. I'd developed a crippling addiction to African things, and had the urge to buy every decent piece I saw. Soon I staggered from one vendor to the next laden with bags, and whenever the other students saw me I had more in my arms, until I began to resemble a traveling salesman with my goods wrapped around me.

At lunch we ate *benachin* in the hotel courtyard, devouring a pile of rice topped by a fish that flavored the entire thing with succulent aromas. With some reluctance I staggered from the table and wandered into the afternoon, picking my way between the crowded houses by myself, or with other students as we came together or went our separate ways. I found a yellow mosque by the water's edge, the source of the call I'd heard all day, looking like a Spanish fort except for the star and crescent on its towers. I peered up at it, hoping for an epiphany, but there was nothing, so I turned and went to buy a shirt that would make Liberace blush.

The artist residences still called to me from where they hung silently above the charging surf, and late in the day I stood on the edge, looking down and wondering how to get down there. I briefly considered leaping from the cliff to a sheep pen below, but it seemed unlikely the sheep would break my fall. It also seemed perfectly reasonable that I could get anywhere other people did, and clearly somebody had a way down there. Those were sheep after all, and African sheep aren't renowned for their climbing abilities. Goats may be able to scale cliffs, but sheep need a path.

An alley at the end of the Rue des Baobabs proved to be the answer, though it was barely an alley at all, more a crack between the cliff and the compounds pressed against it. I followed it down with a few of the girls, sliding on loose stones until the ground fell away to the sea, rocky and broken where the sheep regarded us silently, wondering what we were doing. The place looked ragged. Someone had nailed a machete to a tree stump, and now it pointed its rusty blade askance at the sky; twisted statues and cacti clung to the rocks, and the cacti littered the path with spines that caught in the bottom of my foot, pinching painfully with every step.

In a cleft in the rocks, a shack of corrugated metal and rough planks perched precariously as the sea surged below, throwing up spray and frothing madly at the end of the hole. Each new wave brought a boom of thunder, rushing up the divide and falling back on the rocks below, hissing in frustration. Brilliant colors covered every inch of the hut. One plank showed an African village, another stars in a summer's night, like a Van Gogh painting on steroids, and a third boasted an American flag. We wondered if we should knock, or if we'd be unwelcome. It seemed like we might be intruding, and who knew what kind of nut lived in a crack above the sea. But surely someone with an American flag on their door would welcome American visitors?

When we knocked, no one answered. The girls tiptoed away after that, but I pressed on. Daylight had begun to fade fast, and I wanted to see what was up ahead.

If it was possible, the artists' houses looked even stranger up close, like miniature houses shrunk down until only the doors retained their normal size. The path wove among them as I walked farther and farther out, edging along the cliffs, all the way to the place where they'd tried to build a bridge. The green ocean surged over its remains, endlessly covering the blackened blocks in their ruined march into the depths. I stood for a moment, looking out at Dakar with my back to the cliffs and the sea air blowing in my hair, thinking that a bridge here would spoil one hell of a view. What was it about beautiful spots that made people so eager to connect everything? Some places should just be left as they are, and never mind the bridges, the trains, and the shiny new terminals for airplanes. Just let it be.

Then I went up, because it was dinnertime and my stomach growled, reminding me that the body needs sustenance as much as the soul. The orange light followed me through Gorée's streets, and above me the setting sun cast stark outlines against the old buildings as artists packed up for the night, gathering their things and pulling at the shutters of their shops while the bougainvillea hung silently on the gardens and the closed gates of evening.

Suddenly a man lunged drunkenly at me from a dark doorway, his face contorted with anger, a long knife in his hand, waving it and shouting incoherently. Adrenaline surged through my veins and I felt my nerves jangling as I skipped aside, dodging around him and half-running down the path, but when I looked back he seemed dazed, unaware of my presence, standing wordlessly in the street and staring at nothing at all.

I knew I'd never hear the end of it if I died in Africa. But as I walked down to meet my friends for dinner I realized that could happen anywhere — New York, Los Angeles, or some backwoods with banjo music playing. Danger was a universal constant, a part of living, and even if it was a cliché, the danger made me feel more alive.

We ate again at the restaurant by the pier, and after the long day of climbing over rocks it took the others' leftovers to make my stomach stop growling. Even when it quieted down, I lingered at the table, knowing this was one of the last times we would all be together. In a week we would separate and go back to the States, and it felt as if this were a final punctuation mark on the story of our journey.

But there was still a bit more to be written. The ferry arrived while we ate our meal, blowing its horn as it sidled up to the dock and opened its doors to the crowd on the pier. The bustling mass surged aboard and the ferry left, chugging slowly into the distance and disappearing around the island's rocky bulk, leaving the pier empty of all but a few lone souls staring out to sea. Bill, Debbie, Mary, and I sat at the table for a long time after the others left, watching the island go dark as the sun went down, and after it set we wandered out on the pier, unwilling to give up the night and turn back to the hotel. Words and laughter drifted softly out over the water, but for the most part we were silent, staring up at the stars, and there were more of them than

I'd ever seen.

• • •

The next day ended our stay on Gorée. Early in the morning we left the island and drove south toward the Friendship, our driver playing a single mix tape, blasting American hip-hop through the scratchy speakers as monstrous machines lumbered along the broken road, kicking up clouds of dust that obscured everything.

We stopped for ice cream at a shop in Senegal — just a cement box with a hole in the wall — and a man in a winter coat approached us. He spoke no English, and we didn't understand a word he said, but despite our lack of any mutual language, he wanted something from us. He smelled like he hadn't bathed in weeks, and kept opening a crumpled scrap of paper, thrusting it at us and pointing at indecipherable scribbles inside. We shrugged, but the man was deranged, and we were glad to be rid of him when we left.

The rest of the trip passed like the drive up to Dakar, rough streets with off-road detours, small dusty towns filled with beggars and hawkers who surrounded the van at every stop. An endless horizon stretched ahead of us, and a ceiling of pure blue rose above it. There is no sky like the one in Africa. Nothing really stood out to add significance to the day, and it wasn't until we reached the Friendship that I noticed the date. It was July fourth. Independence Day had come and gone without fanfare, just another day — but in Africa.

## CHAPTER SIXTEEN
# Brothers and Sisters

Banjul, Banjul, Banjul," screamed the tout of the large red van, perched precariously on the passenger door as it hurtled toward me on the morning of the fifth. With my outstretched arm and pale skin, I was a clear target for any taxis, and this one was going my way.

It skidded to a stop and I hopped on, handing the tout my fare as I looked around, pleased with what I saw. The seats were clean, the door slammed shut behind me, the tout didn't have to hold it shut, and the windshield wasn't cracked from head-on collisions with goats.

Bush taxis were the reason my parents blanched when I first announced plans to go to the Gambia. Well, they were one of the reasons, mixed in somewhere with malaria, coups, and the fact that I had never been abroad by myself. But now I was an experienced traveler, a veteran of countless bush taxi rides, and though I had a taste for them, I had to admit they suffered from a few minor quirks. The hurtling vans were unsafe at any speed, piloted by maniacs and packed in a way that seemed to defy the laws of physics. They were the third-string rejects of the automobile world and a wonder of modern engineering — if only because you wonder how they keep going. Then you wonder why you're getting into one of these death traps, but it's too late — you've already paid the fare, and if you get out now you'll not only lose that, but be left in the middle of an alarmingly empty and sunny expanse. Then you'll have to thumb a ride with the next taxi that comes along, possibly in half an hour, possibly tomorrow. So you might as well strap yourself in and hold on.

Only there's nothing to strap in with, because any seatbelts the thing once had were long ago removed, in keeping with bush taxi law. This states that the customer is always at risk, which is also the drivers' motto. You can't hold on either, because your arms are pinned to your sides. Somehow they've squeezed six people into a row designed for only four. They would lay a seventh victim across the others' legs, but the women in the van wouldn't stand for it.

So now that you're in, the fare is paid, the door is shut — or at least held shut by the driver's assistant — and it's time to sit back, pray, and enjoy the ride as the driver tries to collect more passengers by impaling pedestrians on the hood. And he would charge them the fare, too.

That was why, when the red van pulled to a stop, I was pleased to find myself in not just a nice bush taxi, but the King of Bush Taxis. I settled in, relaxing while the driver worked furiously to dodge the numerous potholes that littered the road. Outside the sun shone, birds chirped, and all was right with the world — until halfway to Banjul, when the motor stopped dead.

There was no warning, no funny noise from the engine block, just silence as we drifted to a stop on the shoulder. The other customers and I climbed out, watching the driver and his assistant shake their heads in dismay, making clucking sounds generally reserved for the mother of a sick child. It didn't look good, and if a taxi driver says it can't be fixed — let alone refunds the fare, which ours did — then as the song says, you ain't a-going nowhere.

A moment later I was on the side of the road, arm outstretched, hitching my way into Banjul, thinking that you can't judge a book by its cover and hoping that a beat-up taxi, indeed the Little Tramp of Taxis, would come my way. I was done with kings for the day.

It wasn't a taxi at all, but a wealthy Gambian in an air-conditioned Jeep who saved me, refusing even the paltry fare I offered as we passed the statue of Jammeh and stopped at the taxi park by the National Museum. I'd already finished my interviews with the smiths, but still had orders to place for the girls, who all wanted jewelry made, and Baie grinned widely when he saw me.

"Demba," he cried, waving a sheaf of papers. "The government has contracted with Gamworks to build the training center! Students are to go there and be trained in silver. You should come and be an apprentice, Demba. It would be good. Would you like that?" He meant it, and I said I would like that very much, but soon I would be heading home and wouldn't be around to see the center built. Still, part of me wanted to stay and learn to be a silversmith.

I gave Baie the girls' orders and promised to return later that week. Then I set off for Albert market, wandering through the twisting lanes by memory alone, and in the back I found the wild colors waiting, the men and women calling as soon as I rounded the bend into the tourist market.

"Hello," called one woman, waving me toward her stall. "You remember me?"

"Yes, of course," I said, not at all sure I did.

"My brother, come here," called someone else, and more voices shouted for attention, entreating me with promises of "the good price" and "the best buy." I spent the next hour bickering in the market, until I looked in my wallet and realized I had only a few dalasi left, just enough for the taxi ride home. A young man sat on the corner, watching as I began to bargain in dollars.

"American?" he said, and when I admitted my guilt, he

asked how much it cost to go to America. His voice seemed half wistful and half simply curious, as if he'd asked the cost of a particular brand of toothbrush, instead of a ticket to the Promised Land.

"A lot," I said. It was rare that such a short answer satisfied someone asking about America, but he grunted and turned away, leaving me to argue about why I should only have to pay three dollars for a dashiki with pictures of soup cans on it.

• • •

"You want to post the drum now?" said Ousman Jallow the next day, when he arrived at the pool bar with a drum he'd just sold me. Palm trees and huts, lions and elephants decorated its surface, and the speckled hide across the top produced a mellow thumping when I tapped it.

"No, not today," I said. "We're going to the Julbrew factory." We'd been asking Bill for a tour of the local brewery since we heard about the place from the semester students. They said the staff didn't let you leave without drinking a fridge full of beer, and even those of us who didn't drink Julbrew were eager to see the results.

The factory was on a potholed street in Serrekunda, where tanks of beer swirled next to a room of machines that did God-knows-what. Our guides rambled on about the kinds of Julbrew and their alcohol content, all higher than American beer, but the tour proved mercifully brief. At the end our guides sat us down in the "hospitality area," pulled out cases of beer, and announced that we were not allowed to leave until we drank them all.

"How many of these are you going to drink?" said Debbie, smiling when I said I couldn't stand the stuff and pulled out my bottle of Captain Morgan's. The others began swilling, playing drinking games that I stayed away from, knowing they'd be lethal to me, drinking rum while they kept a safe distance from the fumes.

"Are you sure you never drank before you came here?" asked Abby, holding her nose. I was pretty sure, though memory was quickly becoming a blur, and things went downhill from there as we drank for hours, asking Debbie to play the adult and tell me when I'd had enough.

"As the adult here," she said with careful deliberation whenever the subject came up, "I think it's time you had another drink."

I'd been brought up to respect my elders, so I did as I was told. Everyone was pretty far gone by the end, leaning this way and that, the others taking increasing amusement from my attempts to walk a straight line. One drunk proposed that we offer tributes to each other, and Casey immediately stood up to toast me for bringing a bottle of rum to the Julbrew tour.

"To Andrew," said Christina, "for finding the path down the cliffs at Gorée!" I bowed, almost falling over, and passed the torch to Abby, thanking her for advice on research.

When evening fell we drove into the night, looking for dinner in a mass of dark streets that all looked the same, until we found a Chinese restaurant with a menu identical to every other Chinese restaurant I've ever been in. Tonight was a night for familiarity, and I skipped ahead to the drinks menu, asking Debbie if I should order Captain Morgan's.

"If you feel up to it, go ahead." She should have known better, but Debbie was a terrible adult.

The rest of the evening passed in happy laughter that faded as we drifted off to our rooms, and I felt a twinge of sadness at the thought that soon we would all go home. It was a strange sensation, when I thought that six weeks before I barely knew these people, and at first I took it for drunken sentimentality. But as the alcohol receded from my veins, leaving only the happy sensation behind, I thought that maybe it was real, and sat for a long time in the room, cradling my drum, trying to tap out the rhythm I remembered from the Kura Chow performance, the notes echoing softly in the still night air.

I woke the next morning with only a small headache, the memento of a day spent in the company of good friends and a bit too much firewater. It disappeared with water and time, and was forgotten by the time Ousman arrived to mail my drum.

The post office was just off Kairaba, on a dusty street filled with men selling pens and cardboard boxes. We bought brown envelopes from one of the men, cut them up, and did our best to cover the drum, but the bright fabric of its case showed where the paper didn't quite reach, and I could see odd glances as we went inside, where rows of drums waited on the floor: small ones, big ones, all neatly wrapped and ready to be shipped to foreign lands. The Gambians clearly did a good business with family overseas.

"You want to send it where?" said the man behind the counter, looking askance at the hastily wrapped mess.

"America!" I replied cheerfully. He repeated his glance, but drew up a receipt and slapped thirty stamps on the outside, putting my drum next to a pile of similar lumps, all of which had better packaging.

"How long will it take?" I asked hesitantly, having heard terrible things about Gambian mail.

"Two weeks," said the man, already beckoning to the next customer. I hoped the drum would arrive when he said, but would be happy if it arrived at all.

Ousman sat in the shade of mango trees the next morning, surrounded by hotel guards and Kate, a girl who'd come up to us in the post office, asking if I was a Peace Corps volunteer. She'd been looking to buy a drum, and as she stroked her chin, Ousman pulled out one of the largest and held it up.

"No, not that big," she said, and he held up another, about the size of a wastebasket, telling her it cost six hundred dalasi.

"What do you think," said Kate, "is that a fair price?" I saw Ousman holding his breath, and made a show of examining the drum and squinting into the sun.

"Yes," I said. "Ousman is honest, and that is 'the good price.'"

When the deal was struck, Christina, Abby, and I followed Ousman to his house for lunch, padding along the sandy streets near the mosque and back into the alleys that honeycombed Bakau. His house was a typical one, several buildings around a central living area, a banana tree shading a chicken coop, and chickens scratching in a refuse pile while their chicks followed close behind. His wrinkled grandmother tottered out to meet us, grinning toothlessly, shaking our hands and clapping hers together, beaming as she led us back to the rest of his female relatives.

"You can make the fruit salad," said Ousman's mother, handing me a knife and a pile of mangoes. There was nothing to cut on, unless I wanted to use my hand, and the carving knife was of the type generally used by serial killers.

"I'm just waiting for you to cut yourself," said Abby, watching me slice through the mango in my hand. She squatted with the women, peeling potatoes and chopping onions while Christina stirred condensed milk and Ousman's mother brought out a carved wooden mortar — an indispensable part of any Gambian kitchen. She began to grind hot peppers into pulp, her powerful shoulders working as she pounded the pestle up and down, the thump-thump of it shaking the ground. Three of Ousman's younger sisters sat on the bench beside me, legs swinging under them as the older two sifted rice, pouring it through their hands into wide bowls. The youngest just stared, her wide eyes shifting silently from me to the *tubab* girls helping her mother.

Soon a small fire burned on a stone hearth, and the women added vegetables to a pot full of peanut paste. The *domoda* bubbled for a long time as the smell of peanuts and fresh vegetables wafted across the yard. When it was ready we ate with Ousman off a communal plate. It felt like he had welcomed us into his family, and though this wasn't my home, I briefly thought it could be.

In the fading hours of daylight, Mighty and I caught a taxi to Serrekunda, walking the rutted streets in the setting sun. We skirted the filthy puddles and piled merchandise, searching for more "cutlasses" as the world grew gray around us, the evening shades advancing across the roof-tops and stalls busy with the day's last customers.

Mighty told me he came from Casamance, the Senegalese region south of the Gambia, but for now he lived with a friend in Serrekunda, and showed me the house as we left.

"When you go back to America I will go back to visit my mother," he said.

"You miss your home?"

"Yes, but it is okay. It's good to be here too."

That night we found a restaurant in Senegambia, a place with American food and a band jamming onstage. I looked around at my new family, surprised by what I saw. Our appearance had changed, our clothes replaced by tie-dye, faces burned red by the sun, *ju-jus* and bangles showing on golden arms and legs. There was still no chance we'd be mistaken for Gambians, but we smiled more, as if none of us had a care beyond hopping the next bush taxi and finding a good place to eat. The Lebanese owner of the restaurant came out to greet us, the lights blurred, surrounded by laughing faces, and it seemed the whole world smiled with us.

When I finished my burger my appetite got the better of me, and for the first time since arriving in the Gambia I ate too much of the others' leftovers. Stuffed to an unhealthy degree, I finally tottered out the door, my stomach rumbling in protest as we climbed into a taxi and roared into the darkness. I went to bed with the feeling of sickness in my belly, and the sheets grew hotter as the night went on, a fever beginning to burn through my body.

In the morning I rose early and shuffled outside, feeling distinctly unwell. I'd promised to show Zach the Banjul market, and was a little annoyed to find him ready to go, grinning widely as I groaned. I might have turned him away if I didn't have things of my own to do in town, but I still needed to collect jewelry for the girls and say goodbye to the silversmiths. It would be the last time I saw them before leaving.

We stood at the windswept corner near the mosque, waiting until a taxi came roaring along with a tout leaning out the window yelling "Banjul, Banjul, Banjul!" The van was crowded, though not too badly by Gambian standards, and if it hadn't been for the sickness I might have enjoyed the ride. But the road into Banjul did nothing to settle my stomach, and I felt it lurch into the car park by the National Museum. I didn't have a chance to do more than say hello to Baie before I bolted for the ratty museum bathrooms, throwing open the door with the desperation of a man in severe distress. Only one of the two toilets actually worked, and then with a rattling, sucking sound that made me doubt it would stay alive much longer. Trash and feces clogged the other, and I vomited in the working toilet, washed my face in the muddy water that spewed fitfully from the faucet, then vomited again for good measure.

This isn't how I wanted to spend my last day in Banjul, I thought, feeling a wave of self-pity sweep over me. We had a naming ceremony to go to that afternoon, and Zach still wanted to see the market. I had things to do!

Then I threw up again, and realized how quickly illness

brings things into focus. Five minutes later, heavily congested with my stomach still on fire, I stumbled back to Zach and Baie.

"Dorry aboud dat," I gasped.

"You don't sound so good," observed Zach, grinning cheerfully as I glared at him through bleary eyes.

"Ah, he has a cold," said Baie. I could barely breathe through my clogged nose, and my throat sounded ragged. "Demba, you should go home and rest! You need to take care of yourself!"

"No, id's not dat," I sputtered, shaking my head. A fit of coughing interrupted my protests, leaving me red-faced and gasping. Hastily I excused myself and ran back to the bathroom, thinking I was getting too used to throwing up in Africa.

"Here, Demba, I have something for you," Baie said when I returned, pressing a bundle of crumpled paper into my hand. "These are for your woman."

I curled the paper back to reveal silver rings and earrings. I felt myself tear up at his generosity, knowing I could never repay it, and somehow it seemed this was what the Gambia was all about: people with so little, giving so much to those who never knew need.

"Thank you, Baie," I murmured as he beamed at me, and there was a moment of silence. "But you know I don't have a woman."

"Ah, someday. Demba, you will talk to your father about Jambo, about the university?"

I promised, and he beamed again, shaking my hand goodbye. Then I went to go throw up, and left for the last time.

"I don't t'ink we can go to the craft market," I said to Zach, coughing violently and clearing my throat. His face fell and I felt bad, but there was no way I would survive the market, standing for hours as Gambians called "*Tubab*" and tried to bargain. Even the taxi made me nervous, and I decided I'd better sit by the window, in case I needed to suddenly and violently lean outside.

Despite the sickness in my body, I felt a strange lightness, an elation that had nothing to do with the rocking motion of the van sliding out of Banjul. It was a sense that the Gambia had shown me something I hadn't expected. I'd come looking for the exotic, and in the markets and workshops I found it, encountering lives that were far different from mine, so different it was hard to imagine living them. And yet...

And yet it wasn't so hard. I'd expected Gambians to be different, and part of me still saw them that way, the part that looked at clothes, and skin color, and the way people prayed or went to school. But part of me thought they weren't so different after all. They weren't exotic strangers. They were just people, trying to get by and make the best of life for themselves and their families — Mighty with a mother he wanted to visit, Ousman with his drums and his family, Lamin Fatty with children that he wanted to give a better future, and Baie with a son he wanted to send to college. Even the ones I could do without, Steve Baba trying to sell me conch shells and Ami wanting pens for her brothers, weren't different so much as annoying in their own way, like hangers-on in the subway at home.

What had I learned? I'd learned that we love our families, we care for our friends, and now I didn't want to leave. We try to get by, and sometimes we screw up, but mostly we manage, and sometimes we just feed the monkeys. We're only human, after all. The realization made me smile, and I felt better about the goodbyes. If I'd come here to find something different, what I found was the same. And perhaps there was something deeper, a realization that we had a connection stretching back, before race, religion, and country lines separated us, back to when we were simply the latest apes that climbed out of the trees, struck out across the savanna, and got eaten by lions. And for someone who had never truly traveled, there could be no greater lesson than that.

By some miracle I managed not to throw up on the ride to the Friendship, and spent the rest of the morning trying to cool down in the shower, head back and mouth open as I gargled fitfully. I felt better by the time we left for Katchikally, walking through Bakau's streets in the warmth of the afternoon sun, but my footsteps still fell slowly, shuffling in the dust behind the other students. The smell of open sewage made me gag, though there was nothing unusual about that.

Near the sacred pool, the sound of singing reached us, and women danced in the open space among the trees, filling the grove with their welcoming song. These were the women who had come to cure their infertility with the pool's magic, and now they formed a special sisterhood, bonded by common experience rather than blood — not unlike our own new family.

Down in the pit, Charlie and the rest sat half-in, half-out of the green water, ignoring the commotion around them. Ousman Bojang appeared in a long blue robe, waiting until the women finished their song, and one by one Bill introduced us, telling everyone what we learned in the Gambia. Standing on the wall overlooking the pool, Mr. Bojang translated, and bestowed the Bojang name on all of us. When my turn came, Bill introduced me as Demba Gilman, and suddenly I was Demba Bojang, with Ousman smiling and beaming at me as the women clapped. It felt strange, but wonderful.

The formalities ended and the party broke up. Some guests moved away and some chatted, their voices echoing through the trees while the women danced, chanting songs in the clearing, and we drank blood-red *wonjo* juice made from hibiscus petals. The crocodiles came to life down below, roused from their stupor in anticipation of their evening meal, and they waddled up the bank, toothy mouths gaping wide for the fish we threw at them.

"Andrew, there's a crocodile right behind you!" cried Mary as the reptiles crawled around me.

"He's not going to eat me," I said, tossing a fish. It landed in an open mouth, but the croc didn't flinch, just stood staring, its mouth open as if expecting more.

"No more for you," I said, tossing a fish to another croc and feeling good, feeling very good, even if it was a bittersweet kind of joy. We were leaving in two days, and though I couldn't think of a more fitting end to our stay, it made me doubly sad to be leaving.

• • •

Planning has never been my strong suit, and the Saturday before we left filled with frantic preparations as we ran about like ants, trying to do everything at once. Late in the morning we went one last time to Leybato, to see the familiar shoreline with its crashing surf, the rocks and the waves whispering goodbye. Clouds shielded the gray sky, and it was a strange day. The weather felt torn between hot and cold, with a breeze blowing off the ocean but the sands burning underfoot as the girls stretched out and the clouds thinned obligingly, revealing the sun's hazy outline in the overcast sky. We'd been there only a few minutes when the first hawker found us, a fat woman who plopped down on the sand next to us.

"Hello," she said, and her smile widened when we introduced ourselves. "Your name is Abby? My sister, my name is Abbi too. Do you want to buy anything?" She uncurled brown paper packages to reveal the bangles, *ju-jus*, and cowrie shell necklaces we always saw in the hands of hawkers on the beach. The girls looked, because she'd just called Abby her sister, but when they shook their heads her face fell.

Hoping to collect more shells before leaving, I began to wade in the rippling waves, picking my way along the tide line as the surf churned around my feet, pounding among the rocks. The hermit crabs scuttled for safety underfoot, or hid in their shells and waited for unwitting *tubabs* to pick them up. A small man in ragged clothes joined me, grinning broadly with brown teeth, and I walked away, having learned to recognize a man who wants something. I sloshed deeper into the water, trying to avoid him, but he mirrored my movements.

"Where are you from? America?"

"Er, *no hablo Inglés*," I said, hoping that Spanish would throw him off.

"Ah, *español?*" He beamed and showed those teeth again. They looked like they might fall out at any moment. "*De dónde eres? Eres español?*"

"Er, no," I said, realizing this wasn't going to work and thinking there were too many European tourists here.

"Oh you, you are not honest," said the man, more amused than angry. "You are trying to trick me!" He laughed and flashed a smile, that wide Gambian smile, reminding me it was just a game after all.

"I am absolutely trying to trick you," I said and wandered back, past the girls and toward the end of the beach. Before I'd gone far, I heard someone puffing up behind me, and turned to see the fat woman coming at a jogging run.

"I am Abbi," she cried breathlessly. "Remember me? Do you want to come to my shop?"

"Your shop?" I said, perking up. "Is it nearby?"

"Yes, it is just there," and she pointed to a low building at the end of the beach.

The vendors in the craft market hung despondently about their desolate shops, and when I saw their hungry eyes, I felt like a small fish surrounded by starving sharks. But there was none of the frantic competition so common among Gambian salesmen, and I suspected they would hit anyone who didn't share this lone windfall.

Was this really how I wanted to spend my last day in the Gambia? I kept thinking I should be doing something more meaningful, something more exotic, but I couldn't think of what that might be, and after an hour, with arms full of new clothes, I began to suspect I had a problem. Begging off from further purchases, I gathered everything up and left to rejoin my friends. The beach was almost empty under the sheer gray sky, but I saw the others spread out on the sand, watching the surf and soaking up what sun they could.

"Dammit, people," I said, throwing my bags on the ground. "Don't you know not to let me wander off by myself? How am I going to fit all this in my luggage?"

Somehow there were still a thousand things to do back at the Friendship. I tried my best to pack everything, including the cow horn from the market, but gave up before long and went down to meet Bakary, who'd come to talk about tradition one last time.

"When we began the NCAC it was just me," said Bakary, smiling at the memory. "And I only had enough money for a car and driver. We had to go everywhere, to cover everything." I thought he'd done a good job, considering all the history we'd seen over the past few weeks, and Bakary nodded. "But it is very difficult," he said, "because we are building over so much."

We sat in silence for a few minutes, and then Bakary asked if I would take medicine to his brother in the States. I said I would, and we lapsed back into silence, watching the darkness spread around us as the staff set out tables for our goodbye party. The other students filtered in, coming from last-minute preparations, faces worried but smiling, joined by Mighty and Ousman Jallow, who said how sad they would be to see us go.

Bill had invited a man to play the *kora*, a twenty-one-string harp made with a calabash gourd, but unlike most *kora* players, the man came from somewhere cold and northern. He looked like Jesus in a pale robe as he sat by the pool bar, long hair framing his face, playing into the night, and he played beautifully, his hands plucking at the harp strings, bringing out the sweet notes of a delicate melody. The notes drifted across the compound, and I thought they carried sadness, even when the tune turned light and dancing, but we laughed into the night, unwilling to give up the last moments of our time together. We offered toasts, felt like family, and I didn't want to leave. I'd grown close to these people, Gambian and American, in ways I couldn't put into words. It was impossible to capture the spirit of that moment, so I went about the sad business of saying goodbye, and tried not to think about it too much.

• • •

Sunday morning broke bright and sunny, with the blue sky and puffy clouds almost too cheery for words. We tried to wrap up everything we could, saying goodbye to Kawsu, who asked if I was all right as soon as I left my room, hugging Mighty goodbye, packing, and shuffling around the hotel in a daze. Bakary came before we left for the airport, carrying a dirty, stained envelope.

"Here," he said, pulling out a packet of sticky brown fibers. "I have brought the medicine for my brother. You will mail it when you get to America?" I nodded and wondered what I'd just agreed to smuggle through customs. His hands shook as he put the wad back in the envelope and tied it up, pressing it into my hands and telling me good luck.

For the last time the van rolled out of the Friendship and onto the dirty streets, loaded with ten students, two professors, and a thousand pounds of luggage. We waved goodbye to the gates, to the guards and the men selling cigarettes, to Mighty and to Ousman, squatting in his place under the mango tree. Tears threatened to spring forth as we lost sight of it among the dust and concrete of so many half-completed ruins. In some inexplicable way, this had all become ours, and it felt like leaving home.

"Let's sing!" I cried in a husky voice, trying to mask the feeling with laughter. "Country roads, take me home, to the place I belong..." The others joined in. "West Virginia, mountain mama..." The others faded out. "C'mon, everybody," I shouted. "Take me home, country roads..." The air shimmered in the midday heat as we drove past the crowded rush of Serrekunda, out into the flat expanse of sun-drenched land, and the airport appeared in the distance. The song was just ending, the last notes fading up the empty road to Yundum.

Catching a last glimpse as the plane took off, I knew I would return someday. But for now there was just the long road home, and I staggered through the airports, a skinny stick figure carrying my weight in baggage, setting it down with thunderous booms whenever we stopped, sleep-deprived and resting little on the thirty-six hour journey. In Madrid we found the same quiet corner and slumped on the benches in the early hours, watching as dawn crept into the sky and the airport slowly came alive around us. We had another long layover and we stuck close, too tired to leave the airport. Abby and Christina took smoke breaks, and Amanda cried. Guards had hustled her and every other black passenger away for questioning when we got off the plane from Senegal, and now we comforted her as best we could, feeling none too friendly toward the Spanish authorities.

At last it was time to go, to make that final step onto the big roaring jet, cross the ocean, and return to familiar shores. On the plane I changed into my brightest dashiki and pants. My parents and brother waited at the gate in New York, and their eyes bugged when they saw my clothes.

"Holy crap, mister," shouted a man by the gate. "Where are you comin' from?"

"The Gambia," I cried. "Africa!"

And with that I was home.

# AFTERWARD

Except I never really came home. Part of me was still back in a foreign land, under the heat of the African sun, and bound to return.

A few years later, for reasons that have never been entirely clear, I joined the Peace Corps. I can't remember how I came to such a complete reversal, going from "only an idiot would join the Peace Corps," to being one of those very same idiots. Maybe I drank one too many shots of rum, or maybe I just missed Africa. Whatever the reason, I had many chances to recall my boast during the two years I spent sweating in the bush, and I've since learned not to make such grand pronouncements.

In the Peace Corps, I ate everything that was put in front of me, drank the water, and generally did everything I could to ignore sane medical advice. But the practice my stomach had fending off invaders in the Gambia served me well in Cameroon, the country where I served with the Corps, and I was one of the few volunteers — possibly the only volunteer — who never had to visit the hospital during my service.

Despite the complaining I may have done about some parts of the Gambia — the heat, the bugs, and the beach bums — Peace Corps made it clear that we'd never been truly deprived. We had access to burgers, fries, and pizza if we wanted, to potato chips, candy bars, and ice cream. Most days we had air conditioning. There was always a "white man's store" stocked with the alcoholic expatriate's answer to culture shock and homesickness.

They warned us when we arrived in the Peace Corps

that volunteers in Asia come back Buddhist, volunteers in South America come back revolutionaries, and volunteers in Africa come back alcoholics.

"What if we're already alcoholics?" I quipped, instantly earning my reputation. I'd returned from the Gambia a happy drunk, stumbling and grinning my way into junior year at college. The potent combination of hard liquor and nostalgia meant that every night I bummed a drink off my friends inevitably ended with rambling stories about the Gambia. I'd become one of those anthropologists, returning from the bush and relating his stories to anyone who would listen, running away with conversations and leaving my friends looking at me with glazed eyes, wondering what had happened. They warned us when we joined the Peace Corps that returning volunteers often exhaust their friends and family with stories of life abroad. "Perfect," I thought, "I've already been doing that, too."

The Gambia rolled on under the rule of president Jammeh, who continued winning elections with increasingly questionable tactics. Opinions of the president worsened after my visit, and his victory two years later seemed as much by intimidation as popular support. Since then he's been quoted as saying "Whether you like it or not, no coup will end my government, no elections can end my government. By God's grace I will rule this country as long as I wish and choose someone to replace me."

A few years after my visit, Jammeh received a lot of bad press when he claimed that his ancestors visited him in a dream and revealed a secret cure for AIDS. Good sport that he is, the president decided to share this cure with a group of devoted followers, whose ancestors were either less informed or less generous than his. These lucky individuals, having taken his miracle cure, had no need for real medicine, and stopped taking it. When scientists demanded proof that Jammeh's cure worked, a man came forward and claimed to have been cured — despite never having tested positive for AIDS in the first place.

Whenever anyone mentioned Jammeh after that, it was in the context of his newfound madness. They asked what he was like when I met him, and I said that I met the president before everyone knew about him. I met him when he still seemed sane.

Somebody famous once said, "You can't go home again." I say you can go home — if you're lucky — and if you're unlucky you don't want to. If you're somewhere in between, like so many travelers, you go home and realize you've left your heart far away. Leaving all those happy memories, tied as much to time and place as the people in them... Are you really home? I haven't been back to the Gambia yet, but it stays in my heart, and ever since I went there I've been caught between two worlds, unable to become the person I once was, looking ever eastward. As I wrote this book I looked through my pictures of the Gambia, reading my research notes and the journal I kept during those seven weeks. They brought back the sights and sounds, the half-forgotten images that once again came alive in front of me. They transported me back to another time and place, a small corner of the world that was briefly home.

In the end it was the most vivid time of my life, when I felt more alive than ever before or since. The pictures stick in my memory, and in my mind are always the bright flowers of the sacred crocodile pool, the blue of the ocean at Leybato, and the smiles of my friends on the Smiling Coast.

# GLOSSARY

Alkalo – Village chief, traditionally asked for permission to stay in his domain. Don't forget to bring kola nuts.

Anthropologist – A nut who studies culture, often by squatting in the bush.

Ataaya – A heavily sweetened green tea, used as a social drink and typically served three times in small glasses.

Banjul – Capital of the Gambia; originally Bathurst, administrative center of the British colony.

Baobab – A tree with a thick trunk and root-like branches, found across Africa. Legend says it looks the way it does because the devil placed it in the ground upside-down.

Benachin – Rice dish, typically made with habanero pepper, vegetables, and fish or chicken.

Bolong – Tributary of a river.

Boubou – Traditional robe worn by men in West Africa.

Boukarou – Traditional hut, or hotel room made up to look like a hut, often rounded and topped with thatch.

Chicken yaasa – Chicken cooked with pepper, onion, and lemon, served over rice.

Dalasi – Gambian currency. At the time of my trip, one American dollar equaled thirty dalasi.

Domoda – Peanut stew, simmered for hours with vegetables and pepper, served over rice to set your mouth on fire.

Fufu – Staple of West African diet, sometimes porridge and sometimes a wad of flour.

Fula – One of the ethnic groups of the Gambia, a pastoralist group spread across West Africa.

Futampaf – Traditional ceremony, rite of passage to initiate boys into manhood, also used to open the International Roots Festival.

GGSSA – Gambian Gold and Silversmiths Association.

Griot – Praise-singer, hired to flatter big shots.

Harmattan – Seasonal wind that blows south and west out of the Sahara, carrying desert sands into the Atlantic and clouding the sky, often creating a relatively cool season in West African countries.

Jammeh, Yahya – Second president of the Gambia; took power in a bloodless coup in 1994.

Jawara, Dawda – First president of the Gambia; became president in 1970, deposed in a 1994 coup led by Yahya Jammeh.

Jola – One of the ethnic groups of the Gambia.

Ju-ju – Small charm made by a *marabout*.

Kangkurao – West African spirit carrying a whip and machete; summoned by elders to enforce social norms.

Kola nut – Bitter, caffeine-rich nut, chewed as a stimulant and given as a gift; also part of the original recipe for Coca-Cola.

Kora – Twenty-one-string harp made from a calabash gourd.

Lingua franca – Working language or bridge language, used to facilitate communication when groups do not share a common tongue.

Mandinka – West African language and ethnic group; most common ethnic group in the Gambia.

Marabout – Islamic holy man, maker of *ju-jus* and other charms.

NCAC – National Centre for Arts and Culture.

Neem – Large shade tree, common across West Africa.

Ninki-Nanka – Mythical dragon reputed to live in the Gambia River. Treated like the boogieman by Gambian parents, who caution their children that the monster likes to eat disobedient little boys and girls.

Pirogue – A narrow, canoe-like boat made from wood.

Tubab or tubabo – White man, foreigner. Term may originate from "two bob," the typical fee for a porter during the British colonial period.

Wolof – West African language and ethnic group. The language is often used as a lingua franca along the coast of the Gambia and Senegal.

Wonjo – Deep red, sweetened hibiscus petal juice.

Zoom-zoom – Cashew liquor, about 100 proof, probably full of methanol and definitely a health hazard. Drink with caution.

# THANKS

Any book, even one as personal as this, is always a collective effort. *African Summer* is dedicated to Bill and Mighty, without whom my trip would have been impossible, but I couldn't have written it without the help of a great many people. I wish I could name everyone who helped, but that would be another book in itself, so here's the abridged version.

Thanks to Debbie, for rarely being the adult and always being a good listener. Thanks to Zach, for putting up with me for seven weeks, and to Abby and Christina, Mary and Aurore, Holly and Sarah, Casey and Amanda, for being the Fam in the Gam. Love you guys.

When it came time to edit the book, I was lucky to have friends willing to take a look, and I'd like to thank Mike Gormley, who repeatedly read drafts and never once complained that I didn't pay him. I also owe a great deal to Natasha Hollenbach, who read the manuscript and did her best to give me honest criticism, and to Donna Gambale, for editing advice that I tried to take to heart. Thanks to Julia Bates, the one who taught me to write in the first place. All the good bits had their help, and any remaining faults are my own.

Last but not least, where would I be without the home team? As always I owe more than I can say to my brother John, who designed the cover, buoyed me up when I floundered, and told me when I grew overly stubborn. But most of all, thanks to my parents, for letting me go where I wanted, and not sending me to Cuba.

## About the Author

Andrew Gilman is a traveler and sometimes writer who would like nothing more than to see the world and tell a story about it. He hasn't decided where to live yet, and at this rate he probably never will, but when he's in the States he splits his time between Philadelphia and Washington, D.C. When he travels he sometimes remembers to update his blog, Andrewgilman.net. *African Summer* is his first book, but at the time of publication he was writing a second.

81020537R00119

Made in the USA
Middletown, DE
19 July 2018